Library of
Davidson College

THE GHOST IN HAMLET

AND OTHER ESSAYS IN
COMPARATIVE LITERATURE

AMS PRESS
NEW YORK

THE
GHOST IN HAMLET
AND OTHER ESSAYS IN
COMPARATIVE LITERATURE

BY

MAURICE FRANCIS EGAN, LL.D.

PROFESSOR OF ENGLISH LITERATURE, CATHOLIC
UNIVERSITY OF AMERICA

CHICAGO
A. C. McCLURG & CO.
1906

Reprinted from the edition of 1906, Chicago
First **AMS EDITION** published 1971
Manufactured in the United States of America

International Standard Book Number: 0-404-02264-2

Library of Congress Number: 70-144602

**AMS PRESS INC.
NEW YORK, N.Y. 10003**

TO

JOHN LANCASTER SPALDING

NOTE

These pieces are called essays in comparative literature because they are founded on qualities in literature that constantly connote comparison, contrast, and the influence of the writer on readers or hearers, who in turn affect him.

MAURICE FRANCIS EGAN.

CONTENTS

		PAGE
I.	THE GHOST IN HAMLET	11
II.	SOME PHASES OF SHAKESPEAREAN INTERPRETATION	49
III.	SOME PEDAGOGICAL USES OF SHAKESPEARE	79
IV.	LYRISM IN SHAKESPEARE'S COMEDIES	111
V.	THE PUZZLE OF HAMLET	139
VI.	THE GREATEST OF SHAKESPEARE'S CONTEMPORARIES	171
VII.	IMITATORS OF SHAKESPEARE	201
VIII.	THE COMPARATIVE METHOD IN LITERATURE	235
IX.	A DEFINITION OF LITERATURE	267
X.	THE EBB AND FLOW OF ROMANCE	293

THE GHOST IN HAMLET

The Ghost in Hamlet and other Essays

THE GHOST IN HAMLET

THE number of questions raised by Shakespeare's "Hamlet" have been legion; but there can be no question as to the remote source of the play. It was the "Historie of Hamblet," attributed to Saxo Grammaticus, who wrote it as a chapter in the history of Denmark. It was translated into French by Belleforest, and "imprinted" in English "by Richard Bradocke, for Thomas Pauier," at his shop "in Cornehill, neere to the Royall Exchange," London, 1608. To students who yearn to get at the meaning of the play, who are more interested in Shakespeare's work than in what he read or knew, it is of little moment whether he found the story of Hamlet in French or in English, or whether he drew it from an older drama than the one we find in the first and second quartos and the first folio. "The play's the thing."

It is quite evident that Shakespeare's Hamlet owes almost everything, except illumination, the inexplicable synthetic quality of genius, to the "Historie of Hamblet." A careful comparison will show this, though it will reveal the marvellous transformation which mere material takes in the hand of the artist; as an example of the relations of the chronicler to the poet, the power of compilation to that of imaginative synthesis, and life to literature, it is even more apt than the study of the "Morte Arthure" of Sir Thomas Malory in comparison with the "Idyls of the King."

There can be no doubt that "Hamlet" is the study of a mind, a study, — it seems absurd at this time in the life of the Tragedy to use an adjective to qualify it, — a consummate study of a very delicate yet not unbalanced mind. But since Goethe wrote, after the faint praise of Dryden and the neglect of so many years, it has been so much the fashion to strive to reach beyond this complete and adequate study, that those of the public who read about Shakespeare without reading his works are justified in concluding that the author of "Hamlet" neglected his duty in not leaving a "key" to it. [We have every reason to believe that the Elizabethans understood "Hamlet"; that they desired no lecturers to explain it before the scene at Elsinore opened; that it was not in their opinion a problem play. Why, then, should it be in our time obscure to so many who express such unbounded and even ecstatic love for it? The motive and the action are entirely clear when not mutilated in their expression to suit the demands of the modern theatre. Naturally, a change has taken place in the point of view.] Auditors of to-day do not look on the divinity that formerly hedged a king as a quality of daily life, but they expect in literature and on the stage a condition of virtue and self-sacrifice — altruism is the word — which is not usual in their thoughts in dealing with their everyday relations with their neighbors. For instance, the millionaire who forecloses a mortgage on the land of a struggling farmer is a monster in a novel or on the stage, and poetry shudders at him; but in real life he dines with other persons who have hurled murderers to justice, pleaded in court for the vengeance of the law upon lesser offenders, and who would not hesitate to shoot in hot or cold blood the insulters or injurers of their fathers, mothers, wives, or children. Of Hamlet the Prince, whose father has been killed foully, whose mother has been stained and degraded in sight of his people, whose kingdom has been usurped, even by the election of the corrupt nobles and the connivance of that demoralized mother, the auditors of to-day demand, as a matter of course, an excessive altruism based on Christian principles seldom applied in modern life to actual conditions. Hamlet's plain duty, in the tragedy, is to obey the command of his father's spirit. The Elizabethans saw it in this way. It was clear, according to their ethics, that Hamlet's struggle was a struggle against duty, not a virtuous doubt as to whether it was right for him to destroy the clever, kingly, unscrupulous, and subtle villain whose sin in marrying his brother's wife, coupled with the rumor of a more horrible and secret crime, darkened and threatened to curse the whole State of Denmark. Miss Fredericka Beardsley Gilchrist, in a remarkably frank and original interpretation of "The True Story of Hamlet and Ophelia,"[1] says of the reader of Shakespeare:

"He must be ready to believe that Shakespeare's text contains all the material needed to make the play intelligible, and he must seek for the meaning of the text, without considering what this or that commentator thinks about it. At the same time he must remember that playgoers of Shakespeare's day probably comprehended the drama perfectly, for they possessed a help to its understanding which we have not, — the actors who portrayed it knew what Shakespeare intended them to portray. This the modern student must discern for himself, remembering always that the text, unless it has been hopelessly distorted, is subject to the same interpretation now as then."

The modern student receives, as a rule, very little help from the modern actor,

[1] Boston: Little, Brown, & Co., 1889.

who arranges Shakespeare's plays to suit his special powers, and who does not hesitate to "adapt" speeches and to cut out such passages as he chooses. It is not to the theatre that the student must go for aid, but to "Hamlet" itself, as seen in the text collated by the help of the two quartos and the first folio. He will find certain inconsistencies, some merely apparent because of his lack of ability to project himself into Elizabethan and Jacobean England. This lack of ability is not confined to the student, but to the commentators whom he, often in spite of his own better judgment, or rather his instinct, follows.

One of the most flagrant examples of this blind following of the opinions of others is shown in the varying comments on the position of the Ghost, — a most important one in "Hamlet." It did not surprise the English of the beginning of the seventeenth century that the murdered King should come from the state of purgation in which many Englishmen still believed. It is impossible to kill the vital beliefs of a nation by mere edicts; and the announcement of King Hamlet that he had been murdered without chance of confession, with his sins upon his soul, did not imply, as it would have implied to the Puritan mind, that he was either in heaven or hell. He was in the middle state, suffering terribly, knowing, too, that his beloved kingdom of Denmark was in the grip of a monstrous usurper, and that, if his son were not awakened to the danger of the moment, his dynasty must pass, perhaps forever, from the throne. The auditors, in Shakespeare's time, took the Ghost seriously. He was not merely a piece of perfunctory stage machinery; he was the better part of a good man — not a saintly man — and of a noble king. He had sinned, but he had not died in mortal sin; he was suffering in purging fire, with the torment of an awful secret upon him, foreknowing that, as a king and a patriot, he ought to reveal this secret to the Prince, his son. He must be mute by day, but at night he may speak, and he may not reveal too much. Let us observe how the mission and message of the Ghost are, as a rule, treated. King Hamlet is "necessary to the play," and that is all! The Ghost is a stock figure in the dramas of the group of writers to which Shakespeare belonged, and that is all! He demands revenge from a son too moral and "modern-minded" to accept his dictum of spirit, and that is all. These conclusions are either frivolous or foolish. And yet, unless the character of the Ghost be made consistent with the Christian traditions of the time, they must be accepted. If we accept them, the drama becomes both frivolous and foolish; but as it is one of the most solemn and sublime emanations of human genius, they cannot be accepted.

The Ghost is not a mere theatrical figure. Hamlet is not a modern altruist, analyzing his mind from the point of view of Mr. Henry James and frightened by the bloodthirsty demands of his father. King Hamlet had been a creature of flesh and blood, and he spoke in deadly earnest, for the salvation of his kingdom, for the punishment of sin, to his son, the heir of that kingdom, the Prince of Denmark, who on his mother's death would be king. That other theory, that the Ghost was an illusion, is dispersed very carefully in the beginning of the play. With his usual skill in making the intention of the situation clear, Shakespeare converts

Horatio from a doubter to a believer fully convinced. The Ghost might be the illusion of an overwrought mind, in the awful scene between the mother and son, when the example of Nero and Agrippina is only too near Hamlet's vengeful mind; but the whole spirit of the tragedy is against that supposition. Whatever might be said in its favor should, however, be considered; but the letter, the meaning, the movement of all the scenes in " Hamlet" leading to the revelation of the betrayed and assassinated King, in whose person the whole State of Denmark was betrayed and assassinated, show that the Ghost was a spirit, waiting, in suffering, to be cleansed of the stains of earth.

Saxo Grammaticus wrote the story of Hamlet in the twelfth century; the French translation appeared in 1570; the only edition we have of the English translation is put in 1608. Dr. Furnivall, in his preface to the "Leopold" Shakespeare, says, " We know well how all Scandinavian legend and history are full of the duty of revenge for a father's murder." This, however, would not have been enough to prevent the mission and message of the Ghost from shocking the moral sensibilities of the English people, who loved to read "Hamlet," as we see by the number of printed editions, as well as to see it acted. The scene was not put in a pagan time, the sentiments of the play were not pagan; the tone was much more of the sixteenth century than of the sixth; therefore the fact that the duty of revenge for a father's murder was inculcated in Scandinavian literature would be insufficient, unless specially emphasized from a pagan Scandinavian point of view, to arouse the unqualified sympathy of the English. It must be admitted that these Elizabethans, like their contemporary Spaniards and Italians, found nothing offensive in a mixture of Christian symbolism and pagan mythology in their poems and plays; but the spectacle of a Christian king, lamenting his sinfulness, demanding the blood of his murderer for having cut him off from the consolations and helps of religion,[1] could scarcely have

---

[1] Cut off even in the blossoms of my sin,
Unhousel'd, disappointed, unaneled,
No reckoning made, but sent to my account
With all my imperfections on my head :
O, horrible ! O, horrible ! most horrible !

pleased auditors who were neither irreverent nor unintelligent, nor does anything in Shakespeare's work warrant the supposition that he would have presented such a contradiction. It has been suggested that Shakespeare's " Hamlet," following the " Historie of Hamblet," mixed the pagan with the Christian in matters more essential than mythological allusions; and it is true that the Hamblet of Saxo Grammaticus and Belleforest had two wives; but then, his chronicler says, he had not yet received the light of the Gospel. The chronicler admires the Prince of Denmark extremely, though he was not a Christian, and he excuses his vengeance wreaked on his uncle Fengon (Shakespeare's Claudius) by examples from the Old Testament:

"If vengeance euer seemed to haue any shew of iustice, it is then, when pietie and affection constraineth vs to remember our fathers uniustly murdred, as the things wherby we are dispensed withal, & which seeke the means not to leaue treason and murther vnpunished: seeing Dauid a holy & iust king, & of nature simple, courteous and debonaire, yet when he dyed he charged his sonne Salomon (that succeeded him in his throane) not to suffer certaine men that had done him iniurie to escape vnpunished: Not that this holy King (as then readie to dye, and to giue account before God of all his actions) was carefull or desirous of reuenge, but to leaue this example vnto us, that where the Prince or Country is interessed, the desire of reuenge cannot by any meanes (how small soeuer) beare the title of condemnation, but is rather commendable and worthy of praise: for otherwise the good kings of Iuda, nor others had not pursued them to death, that had offended their predecessors, if God himselfe had not inspired and ingrauen that desire within their hearts. Hereof the Athenian laws beare witnesse, whose custome was to erect Images in remembrance of those men that, reuenging the iniuries of the Common wealth, boldly massacred tyrants and such as troubled the peace and welfare of the Citizens."

This is the apology of a Christian chronicler for a pagan prince, in which reasons of state, as well as filial piety, are cited. But the means by which Shakespeare's Hamlet discerns the murder and incest committed by his uncle are different from those named in the " Historie of Hamblet." No ghost appears in the " Historie," though it is hinted that

Hamblet the pagan was wise in divination, and that "it would seem miraculus yt Hamblet shold divine in yt sort, which often prooued so true (yt as I said before,) the diuel had not knowledge of things past, but to grant it he knoweth things to come," — this Hamblet having been instructed in the devilish art whereby "the wicked spirit abuseth mankind, and advertiseth him, (as he can) of things past."

In Shakespeare's "Hamlet" no such education in deviltry is suggested. Hamlet has thought deeply at Wittenberg, where free thought was the fashion, but he has not attempted, like Benvenuto Cellini, to raise spirits. And Shakespeare fills the Ghost with so much pathos, with such nobility, that it is evident that the spirit speaks not to deceive; he has no connection with the arts of the devil, though at times his son doubts him. To the eyes of the Christian, — let us take the position of the translators of the "Historie," for example, — the spectacle of a Christian son urged to personal vengeance by a Christian father, who hopes for heaven, would be abhorrent; and the

Elizabethans, who, if we may judge by the dramas they loved best, insisted on high ideals, would not have tolerated it. Whatever may be said of the drama in general, one thing is certain, — the successful play must have the sympathy of the audience. It is certain, then, that "Hamlet," one of the most successful of Shakespeare's plays, had that sympathy; and that Shakespeare deliberately maintained it by exalting the mission of the Ghost to the utmost is equally certain.

In the "Historie," Geruth — the Gertrude of "Hamlet" — has fallen before her husband's death; her crime is "incestuous," as it is with Shakespeare, who permits us to believe that Gertrude did not sin until after her husband's death. It is the same crime that Henry VIII, in his delicate scrupulosity, insisted that he had committed because his brother Arthur had been husband to Queen Katharine. The matter needed no explanation to the citizens of London under Elizabeth or James I. The whole subject had been, and still was, a matter of moment concerned much with the state of the realm.

Both Church and State in England still held the Catholic traditions about marriage, though they had ostensibly rejected its sacramental character. The sin of Claudius and the Queen, the corruption of the court, the melancholy of the young Hamlet, the evil rumors of the taking off of the King, — all these things prepared men's minds for strange apparitions, and even the valiant soldiers guarding the court were expectant that some solemn or horrible event, on which they had brooded during long winter nights, would happen, betokening evil, at Elsinore.

The soldiers, who fear nothing of flesh and blood, tremble at every shadow. There has been talk of a walking spirit, — the spirit of a righteous king fearing some ill that threatens his kingdom. Francisco is on guard, just before the dawn, on this night in the late Winter. Mystery is in the air. The kingdom is alive with warlike preparations. Are the people about to rise against Claudius, who has wedded his brother's wife with unseemly and indecent haste, and been named king, doubtless at her request, with equally indecent haste?

The Prince Hamlet, bereft of his rightful place, has proposed to lead no revolt (this his few intimates about the court knew), though many outside who love him would be ready to follow him. There are many, indeed, out of and in the court, ready to rid the country of the politic Claudius, who holds his throne by diplomacy and the favor of the Queen. Thinking of what may happen in this sin-stained land, — for <u>the marriage of Claudius and the Queen is incestuous, not only in the minds of the Danes, but in the minds of the auditors in London,</u> — Francisco stands, waiting for the guard to relieve him. Bernardo comes, and just then there is no glimpse of the moon through the darkened air. He is afraid of no earthly thing; but the figure of the sentinel panoplied in guise of war — for so King Hamlet has appeared — startles him. Instead of waiting for his comrade's challenge, he calls out, almost tremulously, "Who's there?" Francisco rebukes this breach of military usage. "Nay, answer *me*," he calls; "stand and unfold yourself." Much relieved by the sound of this human voice, he answers naturally,

"Long live the King!" To which Francisco, who has doubtless had his own fears, says doubtfully:

Bernardo?
  Ber. He!

Francisco, no longer doubting, praises his promptness. Bernardo, the man on duty, says, with a sigh,

'T is now struck twelve; get thee to bed, Francisco.
  Fran. For this relief much thanks; 't is bitter cold,
And I am sick at heart.

Bernardo is not heartened by this; he knows that the fear neither of battle nor of sudden death ever made Francisco sick at heart, but there are things not of earth that make the bravest heart sick at thoughts of them. He does not want to be alone. He asks Francisco, on his way to bed, to hasten the coming of the companions of his watch, Horatio and Marcellus. Happily, they arrive before Francisco goes away. Marcellus asks Bernardo at once about the Ghost, which is uppermost in all their minds, except in that of the well-balanced Horatio. Bernardo is glad to say that he has seen nothing; and here Shakespeare makes sure that the auditors shall understand that the Ghost is no illusion. "Tush, tush, 't will not appear," the doubting but tolerant Horatio says. It does appear, however. Horatio trembles and looks pale.

> Before my God, I might not this believe
> Without the sensible and true avouch
> Of mine own eyes.

Horatio is not a man to be easily deceived. At every opportunity Shakespeare takes occasion to show that. Another thing that Shakespeare makes plain by every possible emphasis is that King Hamlet comes not so much on a personal mission as on a mission for the salvation of Denmark. He comes as the Royal Dane, the defender of his kingdom, clad in all the panoply of a warrior king; he bears the truncheon, the symbol of kingly power, — not "in his habit as he lived" as man, — not as he slept in the garden after dinner, or as he had jested with his little son and Yorick. He does not come in the easy garb in which he was murdered, to show himself to Hamlet disfigured

by the poison and to excite his anger.
The State is wounded in his royal person.
To paraphrase Louis XIV, "L'état, c'est
lui." In striking him Claudius had struck
down religion, truth, loyalty, the very
essence and flower of law and order. He
was the anointed king of the Danes, as
James I was the anointed king and lord
of the Britons, — and the Britons were
not permitted to forget that the chrism
had touched that royal brow. It was not
necessary to explain the situation to them.
It was the sacred right and duty of a most
Christian king to put upon his heir the
burden of justice. Vengeance might be
the term used, but it was vengeance in the
Scriptural sense, " Vengeance is mine, saith
the Lord, I will repay." The murdered
king had no need to summon a jury; he
was the instrument of the Lord; vindictive justice was righteous justice. Bound
for his sins to silence, he suffers more
than the agony of the purging fire, and
when his chance comes, the king and the
man, the patriot and the father, struggle
with one another in the ineffectual human
speech he is obliged to use. He cannot
speak as a spirit to a spirit; he must speak

as a man to a man, and he speaks by symbols as well as words. Marcellus asks:

> Is it not like the king?
> *Hor.* As thou art to thyself:
> Such was the very armour he had on
> When he the ambitious Norway combated;
> So frowned he once, when, in an angry parle,
> He smote the sledded Polacks on the ice.
> 'Tis strange.
> *Mar.* Thus twice before, and jump at this dead hour,
> With martial stalk hath he gone by our watch.
> *Hor.* In what particular thought to work I know not;
> But in the gross and scope of my opinion,
> This bodes some strange eruption to our state.

The first — and evidently the logical and natural — thought that strikes Horatio is that the appearance of this figure portends danger to the State. There have been warlike preparations; for young Fortinbras, the antithesis of Hamlet, is threatening the frontier, — knowing, no doubt, of the rottenness within, having wisely chosen his opportunity. As Bernardo says,

> This portentous figure
> Comes armed through our watch; so like the king
> That was and is the question of these wars.

Horatio, a scholar, versed in the language of exorcism, and the natural leader of those about him, makes the sign of the cross before it. He appeals as a Christian and patriot to it.

> Stay, illusion!
> If thou hast any sound, or use of voice,
> Speak to me:
> If there be any good thing to be done,
> That may to thee do ease and grace to me,
> Speak to me:
> If thou art privy to thy country's fate,
> Which, happily, foreknowing may avoid,
> O, speak!
> Or if thou hast uphoarded in thy life
> Extorted treasure in the womb of earth,
> For which, they say, you spirits oft walk in death,
> Speak of it!

The cock crows; the spirit fades from human sight, and Horatio feels that the mystical creature will talk only to young Hamlet.

Later, Hamlet speaks to Horatio of his father, and in his scorn of his mother's neglect of that noble shade and in his tenderness, says that his picture comes that very moment to his mind. He speaks as any sorrowing son would speak; his father is before him, but he does not pretend that it is the spirit of his father. There is no delusion; Hamlet is not insane at any time, and his amazement is great when Horatio, whom of all men he cannot doubt, says, still emphasizing the martial and kingly bearing of the Ghost:

>   A figure like your father,
> Armed at point exactly, cap-a-pie,
> Appears before them, and with solemn march
> Goes slow and stately by them: thrice he walk'd
> By their oppress'd and fear-surprised eyes,
> Within his truncheon's length.

The accent on the military appearance of the King is deepened.

> *Ham.* Arm'd, say you?
> *Mar.* \
> *Ber.* / Arm'd, my Lord.
> *Ham.* From top to toe?
> *Mar.* \
> *Ber.* /   My Lord, from head to foot.

Hamlet asks other terse, intense questions; and when the others have left him, he concludes:

> My father's spirit in arms! all is not well;
> I doubt some foul play: would the night were come!
> Till then sit still, my soul: foul deeds will rise,
> Though all the earth o'erwhelm them, to men's eyes.

To Hamlet, of a fine nature but not of the stuff of which kings are made, the appearance of his father's spirit has merely a personal significance; and his failure — for the climax of tragedy in the play is not the death of Hamlet, but his failure — to understand the high and noble mission of the suffering King is the cause of the ruin that comes on all except Horatio. Horatio and Fortinbras are brave and simple. Fortinbras is thoughtlessly resolute and straightforward; a direct line is his model. Horatio is more sophisticated, — a higher type, — but, once convinced, he acts; once convinced, he has neither scruples nor doubts. The simple faith of Fortinbras gains Denmark for him; the lack of complexity in Horatio makes him the one sane, strong man in the tragedy. Horatio thinks of his country and of his duty to it; Hamlet's outlook does not go beyond his own mind and heart. The horrible revelation of his mother's fall drives him almost mad, for he had revered and loved her as immaculate.

Denmark must be purged, — the Ghost dwells on the details of the foul crime,

— that Denmark may not be the chosen place of "luxury and damned incest."

> But, howsoever thou pursuest this act,
> Taint not thy mind, nor let thy soul contrive
> Against thy mother aught : leave her to Heaven
> And to those thorns that in her bosom lodge,
> To prick and sting her.

Hamlet, left alone, calls on the powers of heaven and earth. "And shall I couple hell?" he asks, and for the moment rejects the temptation. He believes that this is the spirit of his father, King and Royal Dane; but he accepts the mission as one of personal vengeance; he begins at once "to taint his mind" with thoughts of revenge, not only on Claudius, but on Queen Gertrude; for the instant his thoughts are as hellish as those of Nero planning the death of Agrippina. He vows himself — sweeping away ambition, and the love of Ophelia, who cannot be pure since the noblest of women is impure — to vengeance. He is not the Prince, the heir of the kingdom, the savior of his country, but the wronged man threatening to return evil for evil. The Ghost can speak no more to him, for the morn is near. The wounded heart of the man had neutralized the cry for justice of the King; but it was too late: he could say no more, but only "Taint not thy mind." The action was now with Hamlet; and Hamlet,

Sicklied o'er with the pale cast of thought, —

of the philosophic doubt of Wittenberg, — is not great enough to understand. He is "prompted to his revenge by heaven and hell," he says. Fortinbras looks on his mission as prompted by heaven, as part of his duty to a father slain. Horatio would have seen the welfare of the kingdom at stake, but doubt makes Hamlet weak. He trusts Horatio only; he has no faith in the love of the people for him, — that very people waiting, as we see at the revolt of the ever-beloved Laertes, to follow any brave man against the incestuous King. Hamlet hesitates; the spirit may be the devil, who may have assumed this pleasing shape to lead him to damnation, as the evil one is potent with melancholy minds, — and Hamlet fears his own weakness and melancholy.

He must have another test; he must prove the truth of the Ghost, for he is not strong enough to believe. That test he applies, all the while hanging on a revenge prompted alike by heaven and hell. Why should he have coupled hell with the duty of a prince and the sorrows of a son? The Ghost has not urged him to league himself with evil. He has not asked him to kill Claudius in hot blood or to compass his ruin by intrigues. The truth is that Hamlet is not noble enough to interpret the message of his father. It is folly to overload the situation of Hamlet with arguments drawn from the theologians. Shakespeare was not a scientific theologian. In the mood of men of his time, who hoped for heaven and feared hell, it was the duty of a man to bring the murderer of another to justice, — much more so the duty of a prince to bring the assassin of a kingly father to justice. Claudius had placed himself beyond the law, and the pitiful heavens themselves shuddered at his crimes, which cried aloud for justice. As a person, Hamlet might have forgiven Claudius and bidden him go his way and sin no more, as the Ghost charitably forgives Gertrude, thinking only of the salvation of her "fighting soul." The Ghost has no doubt of his right to command his son to punish the monster who has deprived him of his human personality and who is corrupting the kingdom. The Ghost, to the auditors at the theatre in London, represented the State; he was the anointed king demanding justice for sacrilege, providing for the peace of the kingdom, and the life even of the rightful heir. The Ghost does not ask Hamlet to kill for the mere pleasure of killing; he does not desire the loss of the soul of his enemy, though this enemy has killed a king and married with his wife. The Ghost speaks as a king; his woe and agony are poured almost involuntarily into the ear of his amazed son; and, after he has cried out for vindictive justice, he remembers perhaps that he may be misunderstood, and whispers to the Prince,

Taint not thy mind.

That Hamlet's test by the play confirms the truth of the message of the Ghost we know, and that he delays action we know. We can imagine how Fortinbras or even the half-corrupted Laertes would have acted at this time. Horatio would have understood the Ghost's words as bidding him deprive the usurper of the throne and save the Queen from the worst in her. He would not have doubted nor would he have let hate so overmaster him as to desire to destroy the very soul of the usurper of the throne. It would have sufficed for him to know that Claudius was the regicide, the enemy of society, the outlaw, and he would have acted in accordance with the accepted principles of justice. Having received the perturbed spirit as that of the King, he would have doubted no more. Evidence he would doubtless have collected for its value to others, but he would have needed no other testimony to add to the avouchment of his own eyes. As to hell, or hatred which is of hell, or the satisfaction of this hatred, it would have been cast aside. Fortinbras would have attacked the King and his court at once with a band of resolutes; Laertes would have hated and raised the people. Hamlet, doubting still, hates and hesitates. He spares the King for fear that Claudius, dying at prayer, may not be damned; the powers of hell possess his soul; he forgets the noble part of the message. He rushes to his mother to accuse her.

> Let not ever
> The soul of Nero enter this firm bosom:
> Let me be cruel, not unnatural!

His heart has been filled with thoughts of murder, in spite of the strict command of his father to be tender with her. When she fears that he will kill her and voices her fear, Polonius calls for help and is killed, like a rat behind the arras. Impatiently, urged by passion, Hamlet would have cut the knot which he had not sufficient strength to unweave. He is passion's slave; passion has made him tardy; he has doubted and raved, and longed to taste the sweetness of satiated hatred, yet never dared to strike. It is passion or doubt, or doubt or passion, — whichever is uppermost, — that has frozen action. He has killed, and he wills to kill; he is not the Prince seeking justice for a crime against the nation, but a mere individual not even justifying the means by the end; he knows the end is bad; he believes at times that the Ghost was the devil, and he accepts his message devilishly. Out of his weakness he has coupled hell with heaven and earth; out of his weakness and passion comes the murder of Polonius. The purpose the Ghost proposed, as Royal Dane, guardian and protector of the kingdom, is blunted by the sleet of undisciplined rage. He delights in torturing his mother. The great heart of the King cannot endure this; he sees that his son has lost sight, in the storm and stress of rage, of the message of justice and righteousness. Hamlet merely mutters and rages against Claudius; he cries out in bitter and personal scorn against him; he raves; he contemns, — he is a vengeful boy, not a just prince. "A king of shreds and patches!" he exclaims; he knows how to use words. Then comes the piteous Ghost, stricken, tortured, not now in the panoply of the King, truncheoned, majestic, but "in his habit as he lived." He appeals to Hamlet's nobler self, for the real purpose of his midnight mission, and for the Queen.

O, step between her and her fighting soul!

Hamlet is called from hell; under the influence of the Ghost's words, he urges the Queen to repentance:

> *Queen.* O Hamlet, thou hast cleft my heart in twain.
> *Ham.* O, throw away the worser part of it,
> And live the purer with the other half.

In the moment, Hamlet is almost worthy of his father. His speeches to his mother, after the departure of the Ghost, show the Christian in the man; the manner in which he reasons for the Queen shows that when he sins he sins not through ignorance, for a closer grasp of the ethics of repentance there could not be. But he has fixed his thoughts on the mere killing of Claudius, and a mind so over-scrupulous, so delicate as his, shrinks, after all is said, from murder, when he must act, though he refuses to grasp the high meaning of his mission. He is not great enough, faithful enough, simple enough to be Denmark saving Denmark; he is only " I, Hamlet — I, Hamlet the man." He will embark for England with traitors and assassins rather than act; he will intrigue, meet craft with craft, rather than appeal to the people, — a people to whom belief in spirits is not foreign, — and, releasing Horatio and Marcellus and Bernardo from their oath, tell the whole truth to the Danes, who already dislike Claudius and admire the younger Hamlet. He distrusts the people. His mother has failed him; Ophelia has been made the tool of her father — frailty and woman — falsehood and man! He will trust only himself; but he doubts all things, even himself. He thinks of the bravery of Fortinbras, moving on Claudius and Denmark with all odds apparently against him, to restore the honor of his name and country. "Examples gross as earth" exhort him. If he would be royal, if he would be grandly noble, if he could conceive for an instant what his destiny should be, if he could soar above the Ego, if his doubt did not stand in the way of his desiring real happiness and perfection, he would not work the ruin of all about him; for even Horatio's heart must be blasted by Hamlet's failure. Doubt has blinded him; he cannot see beyond his small subjective world; his mind is a kingdom in which he is a mere subject. He cannot be great and he cannot be base. He cannot accept the high and he will not unreservedly accept the low. Heaven dazzles him and hell affrights him, and he is too fine to be content with earth. He knows now the worst of the King and the Queen; he has tested them, and the word of the Ghost is corroborated, and yet he can only say, after he has tried to reason himself into fury :

O, from this time forth,
My thoughts be bloody, or be nothing worth !

The voyage to England proves to him that he must settle the matter with his uncle finally or die. Conscience, speaking to him who coupled hell with a message that seemed to come from heaven, has made him a coward; but now he can act as a man, for he must kill Claudius in self-defence. He had cruelly hoist Rosencrantz and Guildenstern with their own petard. Through him they have gone to their death. Still he talks about "conscience"; he makes variations on the "me" and "my." He has sufficient cause and sufficient proof for ridding

Denmark of Claudius; but he is still
uncertain, although he thus speaks of
Claudius:

Popp'd in between the election and my hopes,
Thrown out his angle for my proper life,
And with such cozenage — is 't not perfect conscience,
To quit him with this arm? and is 't not to be damn'd,
To let this canker of our nature come
In further evil?

Horatio implies that the time is short;
the opportunity must come soon, or
Claudius may strike foul.
Hamlet says:

It will be short: the interim is mine;
And a man's life 's no more than to say "One."

Hamlet, weak as usual, though now he
knows what the mission of the Ghost was,
since he sees in Claudius "the canker of
our nature" and of Denmark, allows
himself to be trapped; he is diverted from
his purpose: he dies, and his dynasty
dies with him. Fortinbras, who believes
and acts, enters triumphant, and the
mission of the Ghost fails, because he
who should have been a prince at heart
was a prince only in name. Doubting,

he coupled hell with heaven and earth, and so, like his nobler father, he died unsatisfied, — happier, however, than the elder Hamlet in one thing only: his last message reached ears capable of understanding it.

SOME PHASES OF SHAKE-
SPEAREAN INTERPRETATION

SOME PHASES OF SHAKE-SPEAREAN INTERPRETATION

IT is with much dissatisfaction that a lover of Shakespeare reads the various essays and volumes that pretend to show what the poet's personal religious faith or opinion really was. Apparently such inquiry soon degenerates into active and unreasonable partisanship, in which desire and imagination twist facts into all sorts of shapes. It is only necessary to examine nearly every modern critic of Shakespeare, including one of the latest, George Brandes,[1] to show that the partisan is always behind the interpreter. Sir William Fraser, generally well balanced, loses his self-control, like the others, when he touches the author of " Hamlet." Sir William says, in " Hic et Ubique ":[2]

[1] William Shakespeare : a Critical Study. London : Wm. Heinemann.
[2] New York : Charles Scribner's Sons.

> "Two scenes in Shakespeare I have always regretted. I think that he transgresses in both the limits of art in different ways; they are to me most painful to read. The scene between Arthur and Hubert, in 'King John,' and that between Gloucester and Lady Anne, in 'Richard the Third.' I can hardly suppose that such a scene as the latter can be true to nature. I hope that it is unnatural."

So far Sir William's opinion is very good; and though eminent men of letters who assume to be psychologists tell us that Lady Anne did just what might have been expected of her, most of us doubtless have more sympathy with Sir William's point of view. Suddenly, not willing for a moment that even a pebble should be cast at the dramatist of his idolatry, he begins to interpret. "Has," he asks, "the idea suggested itself that this scene was put in by the poet to gratify Elizabeth by a reflection on her cousin and rival, Mary of Scotland, as to her marriage with the Duke of Orkney?"

Taking everything into consideration, this makes the judicious smile, and Sir William does the best he can, under the circumstances, by putting the suggestion in the form of a question. But it must be admitted that some of the inferences of Mr. Richard Simpson, of M. Rio, of Mr. Wilkès, who take a brief for Shakespeare's Catholicism, are as far-fetched as this chance guess of Sir William Fraser's, or as the elaborate apologies for his supposed indifference to religion made by Vehse, Laird, Kreysig, or Tyler. The researches and opinions of the late Mr. Simpson are edited by Henry Sebastian Bowden, of the Oratory. "The Religion of Shakespeare"[1] is a valuable and interesting book, apart from what its author tries to prove, and to persons who have already made up their minds that all the greatest actors in the world's history were of the one Faith, either by anticipation or participation, it will be delightfully edifying and perennially refreshing. For there can be nothing more permanently agreeable than to find one's preferences corroborated in a well-printed, well-bound book. The defect in Mr. Simpson's "Religion of Shakespeare," which Father

[1] The Religion of Shakespeare: Chiefly from the Writings of the late Richard Simpson, M. A. London: Burns & Oates.

Bowden has carefully revised, lies in the thesis that either the Catholic Church or the Protestant opinion makes or unmakes a poet, or that either or any other religion "gives birth to a poet." "The Reformed creed was," Father Bowden says, "we think, from its negative and materialistic tendency, unfitted to give birth to a poet." And then he quotes Mr. Matthew Arnold: "Catholicism, from its antiquity, its pretensions to universality, from its really widespread prevalence, from its sensuousness, has something European, august, and imaginative; Protestantism presents, from its inferiority in all these respects, something provincial, mean, and prosaic." It is not hard to admit this, nor is it hard to make manifest that the synthesizing power of Catholicity has gathered all that is beautiful and splendid about it; it is needless to express what is so evident. The austere creed of Calvin cut away from the splendor and beauty even of the Bible it professed to idolize. But human nature and tradition and genius have been too strong for artificial bonds, even for that false asceticism which occasionally shows itself among modern Catholics.

It is assumed, too, by many of the opposing interpreters of Shakespeare, that he was everything but a poet, although they pretend great reverence for him under this title; in reality, however, they strain every nerve to prove that he was a philosopher, a historian, a sociologist, a conscious psychologist, a doctor of laws in everything but title, a politician, a hater of the existing form of government, a conspirator against it in words, a devout and lettered theologian, a reformer, an accomplished courtier, and a hundred other things; when, after all, he was something at least as great as all these fine attributes of man, — a poet. In spite of all protestations to the contrary, it is becoming more and more evident to the students of Shakespearean criticism that the synthetical, inexplicable, divine poetic gift that made Shakespeare what he was is the one factor which most of the learned gentlemen — including Father Bowden, Professor Furnivall, Herr Vehse — dim somewhat in analyzing the lesser qualities. He is in love with truth and beauty, like all poets; and the higher the quality of the poet, the more he is in love with truth and beauty. Writers like Father Bowden, Mr. Simpson, and certainly most of the men who make Shakespeare's genius depend on his religion, seem unwilling to leave much to God. They do not realize that what we call genius is beyond all explanation; but their reading of great poets, particularly of this great poet, ought to have taught them that the more universal a poet is, the easier it is for lesser minds to put what they like into his works. And they seem to forget, too, that history seen from the modern point of view is an illusion, so far as it may be supposed to be a guide to the meaning of the past. This is less true of Father Bowden than of most others; but sometimes he appears to lose sight of the difference in the attitude of Catholics before the Council of Trent and their attitude to-day. It is a truism to say that St. Thomas, in the spirit of the Church, made the great synthesis. And yet many of us who accept this as a fact beyond argument talk and write as if the essences he fixed, and which permeate all that is best in art and literature, were invented by him. Similarly we find

Father Bowden and Mr. Simpson noting elementary moral truths uttered by Shakespeare, which were acknowledged by pagans as well as Christians, and which are as evident in Homer as in Dante, as *quasi* protests against the doctrines of the Reformation. In the first chapter of "The Religion of Shakespeare," for instance, Father Bowden declares that the leading idea in the famous lines in "As You Like It" —

> Tongues in trees, books in the running brooks,
> Sermons in stones, and good in everything —

"is in its very essence opposed to the fundamental doctrine of the Reformation, as we have already shown." Father Bowden has already said:

"There are, broadly speaking, two views of nature, — the Catholic and the Protestant. What may be the Protestant view at the present day is perhaps difficult to determine, for Protestantism is fluctuating and manifold. But the Protestantism of Shakespeare's day was clearly defined. Nature was a synonym for discord. Man through his fall was in essential discord with God; the lower world was in discord with man. The Redemption had brought no true healing of this rupture; for salvation was wrought not by internal restoration, but by mere outward acceptance. Saint and sinner were intrinsically alike. In saint as in sinner there was, to use the words of a reformed confession of faith, 'an intimate, profound, inscrutable, and irreparable corruption of the entire *nature*, and of all the powers, especially of the superior and principal powers of the soul.' . . . The mind of man has grown darkened; he cannot see in creatures the beauty of Him that made them. The will of man has grown hardened; he cannot see in creatures the beauty and goodness of the Lord. Creatures can teach man no moral lesson, for man is no longer a moral being. His freedom of will has left him; his instincts are all towards vice. Nature can only find food for his passions and minister to the vices of his fallen state."[1]

Now, there can be no question that Shakespeare was out of sympathy with this gloomy doctrine; but that it represented the spirit of the Elizabethan reform, or that it was held by anybody in England, except the Puritans, is doubtful. At any rate, it was not exposed in the poetry of Wyatt, of Sidney, of Spenser,

[1] The Religion of Shakespeare, p. 12.

and they were certainly Protestants in the Elizabethan sense of the word. Nothing can be more opposed to it than the sentiment of the splendid "Epithalamium" of Spenser. The Duke senior's speech, in "As You Like It," might have been uttered by Horace or Theocritus, voicing the better paganism, — only we should have, perhaps, to re-define the word "good." Adding illustrations, Father Bowden quotes as against the revised Protestantism of the times:

> Their lips were four red roses on a stalk,
> Which in their summer beauty kissed each other.[1]

This is quite as much pagan as Catholic, — in fact, our early Christian ancestors borrowed the symbolic rose from the pagans, and Milton, Puritan of the Puritans, might have used this metaphor without being reasonably accused of leaning towards the Pope. In "Cymbeline" Guiderius says:

> For notes of sorrow out of tune are worse
> Than priests and fanes that lie.

[1] Richard III, Act IV, Sc. 3.

And this, humanely speaking, is very fine and impassioned. But Father Bowden seriously adds:

> "It is impossible to suppose that Shakespeare really held that the singing of a *Miserere* a trifle too sharp was worse than a hypocritical priesthood and a false religion. Read ironically, the text means, 'You talk of the lying priests and their lying temples; I hold your vile psalm-singing to be ten times worse.'" [1]

Observe the effect of searching through the most vital of poets, note-book in hand, to prove a cause. It means chronic Philistinism. If Shakespeare wrote that very human and exaggerated and pathetic and sweet speech of Guiderius to be "read ironically," he deserves to be deprived of the honor of having written it. He wrote it as a poet, not as a polemist; he had no thought of the *Miserere*, but only of a strain, nameless, full of grief and longing. One might as well read into Ophelia's artless speech to the Queen Mother all sorts of insults to Queen Elizabeth, or into Laertes' defiance of

[1] Page 370.

the priest an attack on the Catholic rules of Church discipline in England. In a word, Shakespeare was a poet, and of his time, which was not a Lutheran, Calvinistic, or Puritan time at all, whatever the Lutherans in their confession of faith may have said. But both Father Bowden and Mr. Simpson will have it that Shakespeare was the one Catholic poetic dramatist in a time permeated with general philosophic and popular opposition to Catholic teaching, and hence these strange and stretched extensions of poetry to fit the bed of prose. Not so very long ago, when it was announced that the last words Lord Tennyson had read on his death-bed were those of the spoken duo between Guiderius and Arviragus, some of us regretted that they were not those of the "Miserere" or "Dies Iræ," and felt that the greatest lyrist of our century had died as a poet rather than as a Christian. But when it suits our purpose, we insinuate that Guiderius had the song of faith in his breast when what he had in his mind, on his lips, was the beautiful chant, as much pagan as Christian, but not rejected of Christianity:

Gui.   Fear no more the heat o' the sun,
        Nor the furious winter's rages;
    Thou thy worldly task hast done,
        Home art gone and ta'en thy wages;
    Golden lads and girls all must,
    As chimney-sweepers, come to dust.

      . . . . . .

    Fear no more the lightning-flash,
Arv.   Nor the all-dreaded thunder-stone;
Gui.   Fear not slander, censure rash;
Arv.   Thou hast finish'd joy and moan:
Both. All lovers young, all lovers must
    Consign to thee and come to dust.

I trust that the readers of this article will understand that I am entirely in sympathy with the authors of "The Religion of Shakespeare" in their belief that the Thomist philosophy permeates Shakespeare's plays and sonnets. The poet was the result of previous years and the interpreter of inherited philosophy and ethics; and the results of Christian philosophy and ethics could not be driven from Elizabethan or Jacobean schools, homes, and churches by acts of Parliament. They were of the essential life of the people, and they are of the essential life of the people still, as the study of contemporary English literature will show.

The poet or the novelist to-day — the publicist, in fact, governed by English traditions — accepts the same system of ethics, derived from the teaching of the Church, as Shakespeare used for a groundwork to his marvels. The ethics of Shakespeare are the ethics of Tennyson; and Swinburne and Thomas Hardy acknowledge their existence by revolting from them. The mistake that modern writers, Catholic and non-Catholic, make is in fancying that the influence of the philosophy and ethics wrought into the very tissue of national life by the Church could be destroyed by the political defiance of Henry VIII, or even by years of Erastianism. The sacramental ideal has lived in the hearts of the English people like the vital germ in the wheat grains found in the Egyptian mummy cases. Concerning Shakespeare it must be remembered that he, as a dramatist, appealed directly to the people; he was dependent on the favor of the people. If his audience had found "Hamlet" dull, or "Measure for Measure" alien to their ideas of morality, all the genius of the author and all the talent of the actors at the Globe would not have saved it. But we find that no dramatic author of the later Elizabethan and earlier Jacobean time was more popular than Shakespeare. How does Father Bowden reconcile this fact with the statement that he was not of his time? If any man must be of his time, it is the dramatic author, who is never the master, but always, more or less, the slave of his public. Again, it must be remembered that the party of reform — in the sense in which Father Bowden defines the word — did not frequent the theatres. If Shakespeare had, being a Catholic at heart, written plays against the sentiment of those who acclaimed him, he would not have been able to build New Place or to assume his arms at Stratford as a country gentleman.

One of the surprising tenets of the school of critics to which Father Bowden, and so many others who draw deductions from Shakespeare absolutely opposed to his, belong, is that every man who writes must borrow a great thought directly from some other man. As if great thoughts were not in the air, as if the receptive and comprehensive mind did not live daily by assimilating noble things that are like flashes from the facets of the truth. Father Bowden makes a strong point against the methods of his own school of interpretation when he remarks:

"Does Hamlet say that there is nothing good or evil [in the physical order] but thinking makes so? This idea is borrowed from the pantheist Giordano Bruno, who was in London from 1583 to 1586, just after Shakespeare's arrival there, and who denied the existence [in the moral order] of either absolute good or evil. Again, Hamlet's praise of Horatio's equanimity, which 'takes buffets and rewards with equal thanks,' proves Shakespeare a stoic. The poet's desire for the immortality of his verse in praise of his beloved indicates his disbelief in the immortality of the soul. His phrase 'the prophetic soul of the world' proves his pantheism, and the duty of meeting necessities as necessities clearly shows his determinism."[1]

As a dramatist at the moment of the whitest heat of the imagination, Shakespeare does not represent himself or his belief in the utterances of his characters.

[1] The Religion of Shakespeare, p. 20.

Hamlet, in his "damnèd, vacillating state,"[1] was a pantheist and almost everything by turns, and Horatio says: "I am more an antique Roman than a Dane."

When Father Bowden insists in guaranteeing Shakespeare's orthodoxy by the speeches of his creatures, or fails to see that it is only the existence of the solid but generally unexpressed dogmas behind them in the author's mind that make the never-absent contrast of the eternal with the evanescent, he becomes as unconvincing as Professor Dowden and Herr Vehse are when they draw their inferences. Commenting on Shakespeare's —

So shalt thou feed on Death, that feeds on men,
And Death once dead, there's no more dying then,

Furnivall says: "This dramatic voice, of course, does not always speak his own beliefs, yet such is his 'saturation with the Bible story,' so thoroughly does it 'seem as much part of him as his love of nature and music, bubbling out of him at every turn,' that I, with some reluctance,

[1] Tennyson's "Supposed Confessions of a Second-rate Sensitive Mind."

conclude that he held, in the main, the orthodox layman's belief of his day."[1]

But the orthodox belief of the day was not Puritanism or Calvinism or Lutheranism, as Father Bowden would have us believe. What it was — what it could not help being, when we recall the fact that the mind and the temperament of men have never been changed in a few years, except by a miracle — is shown by evidence of Shakespeare's plays and sonnets; it is shown by the undercurrent in Spenser and Sidney. Says Professor Halleck:[2]

"Shakespeare was extremely fortunate in having parents who could neither read nor write; we can, therefore, be safe in assuming that the greater part of whatever information his parents had, came from the exercise of their own senses in the experience of life. Their senses would be the keener because they could not rely on books. . . . Herein lies the reason why Shakespeare was fortunate in having intelligent parents who were not bookish. By force of example they taught him to rely largely on his senses for information."

[1] Preface to Leopold edition.
[2] The Education of the Central Nervous System, p. 182.

And, with acute senses and an imagination exquisitely susceptible, no human creature born and reared in Warwickshire could fail to accept the evidences of joy in life. Rural England taught the old faith at every turn, as it does in Oxford to-day, as it does in Stratford to-day. The reform was a bookish thing, though it was not very much helped by the knowledge the young Elizabethans gathered from the Catechism, the Psalter, the Book of Common Prayer, or the Small Catechism. Ritualism, reaction against barrenness of worship, must always exist in a country where the Gothic spire and the ruined monastery and the legend of the Sacramental Presence are everywhere. And all the beauty of the "ruined choirs" and the hidden God were very near to the boy Shakespeare and other boys who were not sodden or perverted.

But no; everything must be drawn from books! Shakespeare must have studied scholastic philosophy; he must have read St. Thomas, or Giordano Bruno, or St. Augustine, or Lucretius, or Dante, or Lorenzo Valla. Nothing whatever is left to that power of knowing the false from the true, that faculty of assimilating the beautiful, that quality of expressing it beautifully, which is the gift of God to the poet, and which makes him different from other men. Ethics that are as old as Homer, truths common to all men, — though sometimes blurred, — which have been the salt of the world since Cain broke the unwritten law against murder, flashes of poetic fire that illumined Isaiah, are attributed to Christian authors, as if Christ had come, not to fulfil, but to invent. Let us remark that St. Thomas prefers, in one noble passage on the joys of contemplation, to invoke the authority of Aristotle: " Comme s'il voulait indiquer les origines philosophiques de sa doctrine, et le lien qui la rattache en morale comme en métaphysique à la tradition péripatéticienne."[1]

Now, in "The Religion of Shakespeare," and similar books by partisans, the example of St. Thomas is ignored. There seems to be the underlying inference that philosophy was discovered by St. Paul, and poetry began with St. Peter. This view narrows and cramps us; at

[1] Philosophie de St. Thomas d'Aquin, par Charles Jourdain.

best, it irritates the scholar, and makes the student, blinded for the moment, when he can remove the hood from his eyes, accuse us of clouding the truth. That religion builds upon the natural cannot be lost sight of without killing the vital quality in him that teaches.

In discussing "Measure for Measure," by far the noblest of all tragi-comedies, Father Bowden, who so acknowledges, talks a great deal about the "teaching" of Shakespeare: he is a casuist, in the best sense; he understands that the truth must not always be told; he rejects the principles of Protestantism that "each man is the sole interpreter of the moral law, as of revealed doctrine, and human engagements are supreme, the oath or word must be kept at any cost"; he accepts the lawfulness of "the use of equivocation when the truth is unjustly demanded." Says the Duke, in "Measure for Measure":

Pay with falsehood false exacting.

According to Father Bowden's interpretation, it is remarkable that in this matter "he should be again found in defending the unpopular and Catholic side." We all know the plot of "Measure for Measure," and we know the trick by which Isabella saves herself,—a kind of theatrical trick as common in sixteenth-century comedy as the long-lost-brother incident was in the melodrama of the earlier nineteenth. The Duke advises it; but on the stage an act which needs defence must always be defended in accordance with the sympathy of the auditors. As to the action of the Duke himself, it can only be excused, even as a dramatic expedient, by quoting the sophism that "the end justifies the means." The Duke, as we all remember, masquerades as Friar Lodowick, and in his last speech he says of Mariana:

> Love her, Angelo:
> I have confessed her, and I know her virtue.

It is difficult to understand how this sort of "teaching" can be turned to account by the most violent partisan of Shakespeare's didacticism. But probably Father Bowden does not include the assumption by the Duke of sacerdotal power when he says:

"That is, the truth and fidelity we owe to some, may be at times only discharged by veiling truth to others. This is so, of course, as regards the professional secrets of lawyers, physicians, priests; but though recognized and acted on in practice, the theory of equivocation was denounced in Shakespeare's time as Jesuitical and vile, as much as it is now."[1]

But if we are to hold men who wrote for the theatre responsible for the intrigues on which they hung their dramatic action; if we are to read profound meanings in time-worn stage tricks, what becomes of the "teaching" of Calderon and Lope de Vega, of whose practical adherence to the faith there can be no doubt? Both these great Spanish playwrights used situations which, taken seriously and with their intentions not kept in view, are, to say the least, offensive to pious ears. The dramatists of the romantic period took the material that lay near them, material that had become traditional in many cases. In "As You Like It," for instance, the palm tree and the threatening serpent, not found in English forests, are mere "properties," as the sudden conversion of Orlando's

[1] Page 37.

wicked brother is a stage convention. Your true romanticist does not trouble himself about facts; he uses them, as an artist uses pigments, for their artistic values. Schiller makes Elizabeth and Mary Stuart meet, to the end that a great dramatic effect may be produced, though there is no record of such a meeting. And Sir Walter Scott's love for romantic effects leads him to invent passages in the lives of the great which are not found in accurate chronicles. Sir Walter, like Shakespeare, has always the ethical background, but his characters cannot usually be quoted as representing himself or the morality which he revered and practised.

Imogen, in "Cymbeline," says:

> If I do lie and do
> No harm by it, though the gods hear, I hope
> They'll pardon it.

Pisanio thinks:

> Thou bidd'st me to my loss; for true to thee
> Were to prove false, which I will never be,
> To him that is most true.

And, later:

> Wherein I am false I am honest; not true, to be true.

George Brandes, whose method of interpretation is similar to Father Bowden's, draws from "Cymbeline" — which they both admire, almost revere — this inference, having quoted the lines of Pisanio:

"That is to say, he lies and deceives because he cannot help it; but his character is none the worse — nay, all the better — on that account. He disobeys his master, and thereby merits his gratitude; he hoodwinks Cloten, and therein he does well."[1]

Nowhere in Shakespeare's plays do we find a character bereft of free will, for even his fools have the power to choose between good and evil; and if we take Autolycus, Shakespeare's chief rascal in "A Winter's Tale," as a fair example, we do not find that character is improved by deceit.

"Imogen," Mr. Simpson tells us,[2] "is the ideal of fidelity, and of religious fidelity, — to be deceived neither by the foreign impostor who comes to her in her husband's name, nor by the ennobled clown who offers himself under

[1] William Shakespeare: a Critical Study, by Brandes, p. 338, vol. ii.
[2] The Religion of Shakespeare, p. 369.

the Queen's protection." Now, listen to George Brandes's view of "Cymbeline," and you will observe that Father Bowden, Mr. Simpson, and George Brandes are bound to put Shakespeare in the right, no matter what he does. Mr. Brandes continues, *à propos* of Pisanio:

"In the same way all the nobler characters fly in the face of accepted moral laws. Imogen disobeys her father and braves his wrath and even his curse, because she will not renounce the husband of her choice. So, too, she afterwards deceives the young man in the forest by appearing in male attire and under an assumed name — untruthfully, and yet with a higher truth, calling herself Fidele, the faithful one. So, too, the upright Belarius robs the King of both his sons, but thereby saves them for him and for the country; and during their whole boyhood he puts them off for their own good, with false accounts of things. So, too, the honest physician deceives the Queen, whose wickedness he has divined, by giving her an opiate in place of a poison, and thereby baffling her attempt at murder. So, too, Guiderius acts rightly by taking the law into his own hand by answering Cloten's insults by killing him at sight and cutting off his head. He thus, without knowing it, prevents the brutish idiot's intended violence to Imogen."

It must be evident that the conduct of life, in these principles and practices, would be disastrous. But Shakespeare, writing for the theatre, strung his effects of character and situation on these cross purposes, which it is absurd to take seriously. Why not say frankly that Imogen, like most people, Christian or pagan, in a difficulty, was tempted to tell a falsehood, and she hoped that "the gods" might look upon it as a "white lie," as she intended to do no harm by it. What had Shakespeare, in the heat of imagination, to do with the "doctrine of equivocation"? As Imogen had a good intention, the result seemed to justify it, and it helped the plot of the play. We may be quite sure that the Elizabethans did not worry themselves, as they listened, about the theory by which Mr. Simpson would perhaps excuse it. Similarly, "the ethics of intention," of which George Brandes talks, would have doomed Guiderius, in the eyes of the audience, had his killing of Cloten not been necessary to the plot of "Cymbeline."

The critic who would make sermons out of songs is becoming a weariness to those who know that the great poet is seldom a conscious preacher, while the great preacher is very often a poet. That Shakespeare's dramas are permeated with Christian ethics and with the philosophy of Christianity, there can be no doubt. It could not have been otherwise, for these were his inheritance, and he was too fine to reject them. They were his inheritance as they have been the inheritance of Sir Walter Scott and Tennyson, Thackeray and Longfellow; but he was nearer the source. And he, having God-given genius of the highest order, turned, by virtue of that gift, to the light, as all great poets have done in their highest moments. That he represented the majority of his countrymen we know, since four-fifths of the English nation were Catholic at heart. As to his personal belief, it is plain, from the number of repetitions of the same ethical formulæ on the lips of certain characters, — who are, first of all, human and dramatic, — that he was the child of the Church, whose ethical traditions the English of to-day accept without acknowledging such acceptance. As to his practice, who of us can judge of what was demanded of the Catholic in the time of Elizabeth? Puritanism, gaining ground, thrust his dramas from the stage.[1] "It was a fanaticism which had found its way into his own home," writes George Brandes. Stratford was a stronghold of Puritanism. His wife and daughters, Susannah and Judith, were of the sect. "Judith," Brandes adds, "was as ignorant as a child. Thus he [Shakespeare] must pay the penalty of his long absence from home and his utter neglect of the education of his girls."

And this may help to explain the loss of all domestic records which, had Shakespeare's daughters not been ignorant, might have solved some of the questions that now force the professional interpreters to draw upon their inner consciousness.

[1] Page 391.

SOME PEDAGOGICAL USES OF SHAKESPEARE

SOME PEDAGOGICAL USES OF SHAKESPEARE

THE use of the works of Shakespeare in schools and colleges is general. No school of importance in the United States omits the study of the plays from its curriculum, and the entrance examinations for admittance to the colleges always include questions concerning the sources, history, and development of these masterpieces. An examination of the courses in nineteen representative colleges or universities — these names seem in most cases to be valued as interchangeable — shows that Shakespeare is analyzed as carefully and interpreted as reverently as Dante is analyzed and taught in the schools of Italy. In England neither Oxford nor Cambridge neglects him, and in France a great change has taken place since Voltaire sneered at him; for very recently M. Jules Claretie dared to put the names of Molière and Shakespeare together and to bind them with an exaggerated phrase from the elder Dumas, — "Shakespeare was the greatest of creators, except God."

The plays of this masterly interpreter long ago found their way into the grammar schools, and gradually they are getting into the primary schools. Teachers of experience, who are either the best or the worst specialists in the child mind, are divided as to the time when Shakespeare shall be introduced into the lower schools. But those whose experience has not hardened them are in favor of introducing good literature as soon as possible, and they fortify themselves with some reasons; and one of the best of these reasons is that fine taste in literature cannot be too early formed. Another reason, almost as good, is that the imagination, that faculty of the soul most neglected in education, should be directed and cultivated. We are cultivating the power of observation, more or less intelligently, by means of the "object lesson." We, however, are by no means in advance of that utilitarian school which Miss Edgeworth,

Madame de Genlis, and Mrs. Barbauld represented over a hundred years ago. Not that we should esteem it an honor to be "advanced," but to have attained the best, whether the best have been reached before or not. Those who can recall Mrs. Barbauld's "Evenings at Home," in which the justly esteemed conversation called "Eyes and No Eyes" occurs, and Mrs. Marcet's "Tales of Political Economy," are quite willing to accept the practical conclusions that come from Höffding's assertion, that "everywhere where there is development, later events are conditioned by earlier"[1]; or with Professor Halleck's, that "if brain cells are allowed to pass the plastic stage without being subjected to the proper stimuli or training, they will never fully develop." Everybody, whether a student of the child mind or not, will go further with Mr. Halleck, and agree that "the majority of adults have many undeveloped spots in their brains." There is a tendency on the part of the educated theorist to attribute nearly all the undeveloped spots to

[1] The Education of the Central Nervous System, by Reuben Post Halleck. The Macmillan Company.

the lack of practice of the faculty of observation. Many of these undeveloped spots are doubtless due to the lack of practice because of the lack of opportunity for practice. Shakespeare's marigold and Wordsworth's primrose are of no mental stimulating value to a man who has never seen either the English flowers or those which we approximate to them in our country. On the other hand, the Philistine by the river's brim who sees only the primrose as a golden-yellow flower, with kidney-shaped leaves and a calyx of five to nine petal-like sepals, growing in the marsh or by the river, does not think with a glow of Shakespeare's Mary-buds:

> Hark, hark! the lark at heaven's gate sings,
>   And Phœbus 'gins arise,
> His steeds to water at those springs
>   On chaliced flowers that lies;
> And winking Mary-buds begin
>   To ope their golden eyes:
> With everything that pretty is.

The difference, after all, between the average man, capable of enjoying only what he sees, — Matthew Arnold's "homme moyen sensuel," — and the man who enjoys intensely what he does not see with his physical eyes, is not in the lack of training of the power of observation, but in the training of the power of imagination. Observation alone cannot make a poet, — though later, Shakespeare and Tennyson owed much to the faculty of seeing keenly, — nor can it make the man of science, who becomes great in proportion to his unconscious skill in the management of what we call imagination.

The purpose of this essay is not to make a plea for the cultivation of this faculty by teachers; for in the breaking up of various pedagogical systems, experimental and empirical, the experienced teacher has learned the need of it, though even in religious schools, where the symbols of Christianity are constant stimuli to the imagination, teachers are not always sufficiently alert to apply the psychological processes of the Church to the development, the free development, of the soul. The purpose of this essay is to consider the means of carrying the study of the best and most subtle works of Shakespeare through all the courses of school and college and university, in the American sense of the terms, and to give reasons why this should be done.

It is the business of education to develop all the faculties of the soul, "the soul being, in some sense, everything." The limitations of this business are due, as a rule, to the gradual atrophy of the perception of the teacher who fancies that he has reached conclusions where he has only attained a condition of growth arrested; who seizes theories the seeming novelty of which offers an apparent support to his paralyzed hands. The development of the imagination applied to spiritual things is common in religious schools, for the symbols that show the relations of the natural and supernatural are everywhere. The sense of sight receives the impression of the suffering figure on the cross, common sense centralizes it, and the imagination, trained religiously, conserves, colors, treasures, systematizes the impression. Thus the spiritual sense is cultivated day by day, hour by hour, and all the faculties of the soul are directed toward a fuller richness of faith. There is no play of fancy about these object lessons, they appeal to no intermediate quality between the imagination and the judgment — they satisfy both.

It is often a matter of wonder that many persons who have what we call "the spiritual sense" highly cultivated have little perception of the beauties of music, art, literature, or architecture, except when these arts are directly applied to the service of religion. Conversely, we have even a greater number whose perception of beauty in nature or art is blunted the moment nature and art are taken into the service of religion; they have neither the gift of faith nor has the spiritual sense been cultivated. That one may exist without the other, experience abundantly shows.

Let it be admitted that one of the duties of the teacher is to cultivate and direct the imagination, and it ought to follow that he cannot begin too soon. It follows, too, that he ought to put within the reach of the pupil such literature as will lay the foundation of taste and culture at the earliest possible moment. It would be folly to attempt to teach philosophy to the very young, because the study of philosophy demands qualities that are lacking in the minds of the very young; but the cultivation of taste and the enriching of the imagination have nothing to do with exact definitions and analyses and carefully distinguished processes. What literature is best for the young whose taste and power of conserving beautiful impressions are to be educated? The sort of food offered to the children in the shape of little stories and articles that are literary prolongations of the odious patois called "baby talk," which must make the most intelligent infant hate his species at the very moment he enters life; the attempts in letters of the atrophied adult mind to bring itself to the level of the child mind with the dew of God's morning upon it? By no means. The child should be prepared to accept the masterpieces. The child lives in his own world. His senses seem miraculously keen until he begins to believe that all lessons should be learned through books, and then the fatal art of printing is set up as a screen between him and the wonders of the world God has given him. One can no more hear Shakespeare without seeing the unspoiled imagination of the Stratford boy than one can read St. John without feeling that the sunsets of Patmos were finer than any known in western skies, — at least they were finer to him, whose imagination irradiated his observation.

The value of the exercise of the faculty of observation, and of the process by which the imagination stores impressions, is nowhere more evident than in Shakespeare's plays. In "The Education of the Central Nervous System," a book of great value to teachers, Mr. Halleck says:

"Every one ought to know how Shakespeare's senses were trained; for in his sensory experience is to be found the formation of all those imperishable structures given to humanity by his heaven-climbing genius.

"Two things are true of Shakespeare, — his senses had magnificent training; the stimuli of nature also had in him a wonderful central nervous system to develop. We shall not reach his heights, but if we have the proper training we shall ascend far higher than we could without it. If John Weakling can never make a Samson, that is no reason why John should not take proper gymnastic exercise, and develop his latent powers to the utmost. At their best they may be poor; at their worst they may keep him through life the slave of underlings. After going through sensory training similar to Shakespeare's, any boy would be better fitted to cope with the world." [1]

Mr. Halleck elaborates this passage by many quoted extracts from Shakespeare's plays. Warwickshire is always present in the plays, for Shakespeare never gets outside the sensory world of his boyhood, and from the treasury of that world come thousands of beautiful passages. The cowslip, with the drop of crimson in its cup, in "Cymbeline," the deer seen by Jaques from the roots of the oak, the action of the water as Ophelia is drawn down into the pool, the fairy-like bending of the pease-blossom, the moonlight on the wild thyme and the musk rose, the eglantine, the swan's nest in the great pond, the marsh marigold, the dog out in the cold in "Lear," the chill before the dawn in "Hamlet," the shadow of the hawk stilling the singing of the lesser birds, the "plain-song cuckoo gray," — a quick-eyed boy noted all these things in

[1] Page 171.

his walks in the most beautiful lanes and meadows and by the serenest river in England. They were stored in his imagination, and when the time for expression arrived they became like illuminated pictures in the text of a missal:

> "Sleep no more!
> Macbeth does murder sleep," the innocent sleep,
> Sleep that knits up the ravell'd sleave of care,
> The death of each day's life, sore labour's bath,
> Balm of hurt minds, great nature's second course,
> Chief nourisher in life's feast.

And Portia's illustration:

> The crow doth sing as sweetly as the lark
> When neither is attended!

On every page in the plays we find the impressions taken from life illuminated in this way, and certainly any training which may so make the ordinary things of earth glow through the conjunction of memory and imagination must be good for the student of any age. But the older a man grows, the less vivid become his impressions, so that the earlier the dramas of Shakespeare are used in the training of the central nervous system the better; therefore a child ought to be interested as soon as possible in the study of nature and taught to absorb the beauty of the natural allusions in Shakespeare's plays. Shakespeare had seen the light clouds in the April sky on Stratford's fields, and the swan's feather float upon the swell at the turn of the tide. And, later, he read the story of Octavius Cæsar and Antony. And when he came to represent the parting of Octavia's husband and brother from her, he makes her say:

My noble brother!

And, looking at her, Antony speaks:

The April's in her eyes: it is love's Spring,
And these the showers to bring it on.

. . . .

Her tongue will not obey her heart, nor can
Her heart inform her tongue, — the swan's down-feather,
That stands upon the swell at full of tide,
And neither way inclines.

The thing seen — the veriest trifle it may seem to be at the moment — becomes part of the imagination, to give a new beauty to thoughts and emotions, and to make life full of suggestiveness. This synthesis between the sight of a thing and the power of assimilating it imaginatively is, often seems to be, a poetic gift, — in Shakespeare's case a supreme and inexplicable gift, according to the older philosophers; an explicable gift according to the younger. It is his alone, and, because he possessed genius or had an unusually live brain, he has produced a new wonder for the world; consequently, his powers of assimilation and of giving out the result of this assimilation were special with him, and, though they may be admired, they cannot be imitated. No student of the soul will deny this. For the pupil it is not a question of being a genius, but it is a question of getting the greatest possible amount of contentment out of life. Men reach toward brightness and rest and change, as the small sapling in the dense wood straightens itself toward the light. Psychologists have said, over and over again, that it is the avocations not the vocations of life that make it pleasant; the means of higher pleasure cannot be too greatly multiplied, then, when life is young. The muscles of the body sleep, if not trained; the sensory nerves and all the delicate ducts of the system require early training and constant activity as well. The memory becomes a precious collection of dynamic associations, if the art of observation and the results of this art are cultivated and pointed out. To store vital impressions and to so employ them that they may add to the joy of life is not the exclusive birthright of the poet, though a Shakespeare or a Wordsworth may possess it preëminently. To-day we are learning to use literature as an instrument in the education of the soul, not as an end; as a means of development, not as an object to which the development of a few higher beings may tend. Every boy or girl may not feel Burns's thrill at the sight of a daisy, or Wordsworth's wonder that there should be any to whom a primrose should not give

> Thoughts that do often lie too deep for tears,

or Tennyson's passionate desire to know the meaning of the flower in the crannied wall, or Bryant's pleasure in the yellow violet; but he may have at least a well-stored memory and be taught that there is an

> Hour
> Of splendour in the grass, of glory in the flower,

and that this hour, assimilated with human feeling or experience, may become a perpetual joy in the memory.

The plays of Shakespeare, then, from the time that the child becomes capable of the process of connecting the things of nature with the emanations of the soul we call literature, are fine instruments ready for the work of the teachers. Charles Lamb, who loved much and suffered much, and who never lost the insight of a grown-up child, saw this; and, seeing it, helped his sister to give the world the little classic called " Tales from Shakespeare." Says the preface of this delightful volume:

"The plays of Shakespeare are enrichers of the fancy, strengtheners of virtue, a withdrawing from all selfish and mercenary thoughts, a lesson in all sweet and honorable thoughts and actions, to teach courtesy, benignity, generosity, humanity; for of examples teaching these virtues his pages are full."

The preface hints at the necessity of keeping the plays from very young persons, and suggests that young gentlemen, who are permitted to range in their father's library at an earlier age than their sisters, should, after careful selection, read certain parts of the plays to them. The demand for supplementary reading in the primary schools has been answered by "The Beginner's Shakespeare."[1] Charles and Mary Lamb tried to retain the language of Shakespeare in their charming stories as much as possible, and their work remains as important in introduction to Shakespeare as that other classic, the "Tanglewood Tales," is to the Grecian myths. The acknowledgment of the value of Shakespeare's verse in developing the faculty of imagination has produced other carefully arranged editions for the young. The mere story, though it excited interest, was not enough, for the plots of Shakespeare's plays are only skeletons, and the arranged words of such dramas as can be adapted for the very young are needed in the cultivation of the imagination. No masterpieces of literature are so well adapted for this end.

---

[1] Boston: Heath & Co.; Home and School Classics.

In the higher schools into which Shakespeare's plays have been introduced by wise educators, and the necessity of their study as part of the English requirements for entrance into colleges insisted upon, several very unpedagogical mistakes have been made. The editions have been overburdened with notes, — some of them foolish or obvious and others so written as to avoid any explanation of real difficulties; and the study of the metres has been almost entirely neglected. I am not speaking of that scientific study which would be a waste of time in secondary or high schools, but of that study for the purpose of culture which would add much to the enjoyment of the art of reading and develop the sense of rhythm. Elaborate notes on "Hamlet" or "Julius Cæsar," for instance, have no pedagogical value in school or college courses. They satiate the interest and cut off all discussion. To delay the reading of a play in order to consider a note that tells the pupil of the Warwickshire origin of "conditioned" when that word is used in Act III, Scene 2 of "The Merchant of Venice" or that "to pun" in Act II, Scene 1 of "Troilus and Cressida" means in Warwickshire "to quilt, leather, or pound" a man severely, and to compare the Warwickshire meaning with that of five other dialects, is simply to impede the movement of the drama. In many cases the aim of both the editor and the teacher seems to be to burden the memory with details of little moment compared with the broadening and elevating of the pupil's mind. The reading and study of Shakespeare ought to be not with the intention of inducing the student to accept conclusions, but to find conclusions for himself. In mathematics it is the process that is valuable to the pupil; in logic it is the process too; and in physical and chemical laboratories as well, the teacher and pupil often know what the results will be; but the processes of the experiment are what the student must learn. The page overcrowded with answers to every possible question, the learned and the unlearned conjectures in passages which might safely be left to the student's own intuition, and the constant attempt to prejudice in favor of a personal interpretation, weary the attention and deaden the power of perception. The philology of the plays ought never to be neglected, but a too minute inquiry into it — especially if the editor and the teacher do all the inquiring — is contrary to the axiom that the student, in all grades, should work for himself, with only such assistance as may clear his path without making it a royal road.

In some of the high schools too many plays are read lazily and without due attention to the condition of English speech in the Elizabethan and Jacobean time. While minute philological details, merely memorized, are detrimental to the progress of the development of the student, certain important changes, particularly the gradual loss of the Old English inflections, ought to be pointed out and illustrated, as well as the various meanings which distinguish modern words from those of the same form used by Shakespeare and his contemporaries. It is very easy to do too much of this. The study of Shakespeare in secondary and high schools must be to the student a labor of love. The moment it becomes perfunctory it ceases to be worth the effort. A good text, a glossary, a facsimile of the First Folio, and an enthusiastic teacher will work wonders.

Students whose reading has been almost incredibly limited will learn to get the best from "Hamlet" or "The Merchant of Venice," and, outside of the mental development, they will soon learn "by the feel," as it were, by the unconscious refinement of taste that comes of familiar contact with masterpieces, to know the inferior literary production when they see it. A man or a woman brought up with "Hamlet" is not likely to speak of Marie Corelli as one of the elect. The purification of taste is a work not unworthy of the best-equipped teacher. The rustic boy, fresh from the plough, whose reading has been confined to rudimentary text-books and the country paper, if he be kept in close association with one of Shakespeare's best plays cannot fail to be so strengthened in taste and prejudiced in favor of luminousness, cleanness, and beauty that he will neglect lesser things. I have observed that, from the boy of ten to the student of thirty,

Shakespeare speaks to each according to his capacity.

Of the hundreds of doctors' theses from the German universities Shakespeare furnishes the material for scores. At Oxford, even, and in the Cambridge Tripos, where one hardly expects to find an appeal to mere taste, he is important as a basis for historical and philological work; in fact, into every department in practical pedagogy Shakespeare enters more and more; but in the intermediate and undergraduate courses one of his chief values is that, properly assimilated, he stands in the way of that mental frivolity and dissipation which, while it demands the multiplication of new books, is ruinous to all concentrated and consecutive thought. "The great religious poets, the imaginative teachers of the heart, are never easy reading," Frederick Harrison says in "The Choice of Books." And Shakespeare, who is the first of the imaginative teachers, is not easy reading from the point of view of the mob that spends half a lifetime in "sucking magazines and new poems." Frederick Harrison further says:

"It is a true psychological problem, this nausea which idle culture seems to produce for all that is manly and pure in heroic poetry. The intellectual system of most of us in these days needs 'to purge and to live cleanly.' Only by a course of treatment shall we bring our minds to feel at peace with the grand, pure works of the world. To understand a great national poet, such as Dante, Calderon, or Goethe, is to know other types of human civilization, in ways in which a library of history does not sufficiently teach. The great masterpieces of the world are thus, quite apart from the charm and solace they give us, the master instruments of a solid education."

Nobody pretends that Shakespeare's plays are all great or all worthy of serious attention, or that they all have pedagogical possibilities beyond the uses of their philology; the greatest of them have defects, but these very defects are so personal, so natural, so much of the time, that even they may be made subjects for pregnant study. But when Shakespeare is noble he is supremely noble. His variety is infinite, and his power of stimulus and suggestion so strong that, once beloved, once even partially understood, he helps us to acquire that force of rejection which

the modern reader, above all things, needs.
The real teacher's motto is, "For the
greater glory of God," and he groups
together all beautiful and great things
about his student beneath this motto. It
is like the cross, as Ruskin saw it, in
St. Mark's at Venice, — the great central
fact. It is often borne in upon him, with
an iteration that makes him desperate,
how futile his efforts are against popular
currents because in early life the pseudo-
student's taste has not been directed.
This taste is broad in the worst sense,
and it accepts the road of the least resist-
ance. It offers no obstacle to the vain,
the frivolous, the philosophically untrue,
or the sensuously destructive. Its delights are those of the dreamer, with no
intellectual pilot.

It seems to be forgotten that good taste
is one of the surest tonics for moral thinking. The teacher may talk as forcibly
as Mr. Frederick Harrison has written
on the value of the great books; he
may declare with passion that a few books
are best, but the popular desire for
easy reading — foi the book about books,
for the thing talked about — will be too

much for him. And yet, we all accept the truth of the maxim of St. Thomas, "Natura autem nulli deest in necessariis"; and therefore the soul has its splendid auxiliary, the body. Why not admit that the education of the spiritual sense ought to have as auxiliary the education of its helper, good taste, at the earliest possible moment? The teacher needs all the assistance he can get from the soul of his pupil, and if the soul be prejudiced in favor of what is beautiful, his work becomes one of progression. It is a truism to say that trailing clouds of glory should surround the young soul, and that its earthly guardians should, if possible, keep the knowledge of evil from it; all the adepts in child study have said this a thousand times.

Let us be practical about it; and if we admit that good taste in art and literature is a desirable aid to the seeing of that beauty which God gives us on earth, as a help to the knowledge of Him, why should we not, from the beginning of the child's school life, keep the evil of low aims from it? There should be no disputing about tastes, in the sense that there is, as regards truly great works, only one standard of taste; and this standard should be tactfully applied. The atheist who would sneer at the Book of Job or Isaiah or the Apocalypse, from the point of view of literary beauty, would judge himself. Similarly, only a barbarian would attempt to displace Dante from the niche in which the universal consensus has put him. But the man who admires the Bible or Dante without reading either or knowing of himself why they are great is a dumb, driven follower of beauty. While Shakespeare never touches the grandeur of the Apocalypse or the majesty of Dante, he remains as the finest interpreter of the heart that the world has ever known. The story of "The Merchant of Venice," full of the interest of romance when we are very young, becomes later a criticism of life, a treasure-house of philosophy, the tragedy of a soul and of a nation. It is the material, properly used, with which the teacher may work wonders for the solace of middle life, for the consolation of old age. In truth, if all the "Rhetorics" were taken away, and the teacher were to use "Hamlet" or "King Lear" or "The Merchant of Venice" or "As You Like It," as physicists use materials in their laboratories, we should have clearer-headed men and women, very easily expressing themselves; for, in English at least, there can be no rules of rhetoric capable of vitalized application which are not drawn from the practices of the masters. Dr. Rolfe has an admirable page on the teaching of elementary rhetoric by the inductive method.[1] Professor Rolfe says:

"In the reading of poetry the essential principles and laws of versification may be taught, the pupil being made to deduce them for himself from the poem before him; . . . it is the right time for learning what children of larger growth often fail to acquire. The young child never errs in the rhythmical rendering of Mother Goose, that classic of the nursery; but adults and teachers, and sometimes even college professors, who have lost the childish sensitiveness to the music of verse, will often blunder in reading or reciting Shakespeare."

Mr. Rolfe further indicates the use of those masterpieces in the teaching of

[1] The Elementary Study of English, by W. J. Rolfe, Litt. D. Harper & Bros.

elementary rhetoric. All young persons use tropes in daily conversation.

"The small boy, who is so much given to similes that when he is hard up for a mere specific comparison he will say 'like *anything*,' making up in emphasis what the expression lacks in point and precision, will not be slow to recognize that sort of thing in the printed page if you call his attention to it. He will pick out the similes and metaphors as readily as the nouns and verbs, and explain the resemblances on which they are based, as easily as the syntax of subject and predicate. . . . . To note and name these figures soon becomes a merely mechanical process — much like parsing, and as profitless; but to see whether the figure is apt or expressive or beautiful, and to find out and explain why it is so, is a practical lesson in truth and criticism."

The material for these exercises is supplied by any of the great plays of Shakespeare. No English author gives, ready at hand, such a wealth of objects on which to expend mental energy. The skilful teacher has long ago discarded the volume of "elegant extracts." It was Walter Savage Landor who, I think, said of somebody's sonnets that he did not like his sentiment cut up into little patty pans. The book of "elegant extracts" may, as a rule, be classed with these mechanical sonnets. But "Macbeth," "King Lear," "Hamlet," "Julius Cæsar," "The Tempest," "As You Like It" may be so used that they accompany the student through his whole life, perennially giving forth new means of enjoyment and culture.

Who has not noticed the ease with which intelligent readers of Shakespeare acquire the inflections of his verse? And when, by practice, the metrical and rhythmical swing of his verse has become a thing of habit, a finer appreciation of all verse forms in English becomes no difficult matter. It has been often remarked that, while the teaching of English occupies so large a space in the catalogues of the intermediate schools, — all those above the rudimentary grades, — and in undergraduate university courses, a knowledge of the musical charm of English verse is exceedingly rare. The elocutionists of the older days insisted that blank verse should be read as prose, and the prosier you made your cadences and the more redundant were your gestures, the more satisfactory your elocution was supposed to be. The cunning music of Jaques's famous speech, beginning " All the world's a stage," was lost, because it was understood that while it might be scanned in classes according to outworn Greek or Latin rules, its metre had no relation whatever to the uttering of it; and so when the elocutionist, struggling to beat the five-accented Shakespearean iamb into dull monotony, spoke of the " whining schoolboy," he pointed to an imaginary satchel, and when he described the lover

> With a woeful ballad
> Made to his mistress' eyebrow,

he touched his own, and only a very nice sense of propriety prevented him from an appropriate gesture when he alluded to the justice:

> In fair round belly with good capon lined.

After many years it has been discovered that when a poet writes in verse he means to produce an effect through the ear, not only through the eye; that when Shakespeare wrote in prose he fitted the form to the feeling, and that he intended that all his exquisite metrical interweaving of verse melody should be given by the only instrument capable of uttering them, — that speaking voice which the pedagogues too much neglect. To what better use can the scene between Lear (mad through pride, adulation-fed) and his daughters be put than in the training of the concealed qualities of the voice? When a young woman can utter Cordelia's words, "So young, my lord, and true," with the simplicity and the musical flow that follows "so young, and so untender?" she has learned more than all the rules of scansion can teach her.

It was my intention to touch on some further uses of Shakespeare in the art of pedagogy, especially where philology and history are concerned and analysis and comparison are so necessary; but I find that I have already made this essay longer than I wished, — yet I have only slightly sketched processes which are with advantage applied to the works of the greatest of all English masters in literature.

LYRISM IN SHAKESPEARE'S COMEDIES

LYRISM IN SHAKESPEARE'S COMEDIES

THERE is a great difference between a comedy by Shakespeare and a comedy by Molière. And this difference is not only the difference that must exist between a play written for Elizabethans, who went to the theatre dependent on a strong appeal to the imagination, and people of the time of Louis XIV desiring to see life as it was reflected on the stage. The age of Elizabeth and the age of Louis XIV were very unlike. The mob that filled the pit of the Globe Theatre had little affinity with the courtiers who gathered at St. Cyr[1] to listen to the "Esther" of Racine, to wonder whether the Count de Soissons was the original of the man who discovered that he had been talking prose all his life, and to insinuate that the model for Tartufe

[1] Letters of Madame de Sévigné, June 12, 1680; Feb. 21, 1689.

was the Bishop of Autun.[1] The real difference, however, lies in the fact that the plays of Molière are comedies, pure and simple, while the most beautiful of Shakespeare's are lyrical extravagances. Speaking of Aristotle, Cardinal Newman says: "The inferior poem may, on his principle, be the better tragedy." A careful examination of any play of Molière's and a comparison of it with the best comedies of Shakespeare will show that Shakespeare was, by all odds, a poet, while Molière was not a poet at all, but, in the best sense, a comedian of the highest order. Leaving out the question as to the distinctly opposite views of life and their art taken by these men of genius, I may say that the essential difference between them is the difference between poetry and prose. And though prose may be not unmusical, yet it is never lyrical, and all the plays of Shakespeare, except in certain prosaic passages introduced consciously, are lyrical; they are

[1] It must have been the enemies of Mgr. de Roquette who whispered this, for the real Tartufe was a certain M. Fertant. See "La Vraie Fin de Tartufe," *Revue Bleue*, May 13, 1899.

full of emotion, mood, feeling, the quality of aspiration, musically expressed. The music of the composer and the music of the poet are not the same, but they touch each other. The poet who lives in a musical time will set his cadences and pauses to the tunes he hears. The air is full of music, and the accent of familiar songs sets the mould for the metres of the bard.

Shakespeare's time was the most musical that England ever knew. The lute and the spinet were everywhere; the madrigal and the glee so common that at any moment in the day voices were ready to join in them. "It was the Puritan,"[1] George Brandes says, "who cast out music from the daily life of England. Spinets stood in the barbers' shops for the use of customers waiting their turn." Music tried to get back with the Restoration, as we see from the passionate devotion of both Evelyn and Pepys, to the part-songs, but it had gone out of the everyday existence of a people who after a while heard music

[1] William Shakespeare : A Critical Study, by George Brandes. The Macmillan Company, 1898.

only as an exotic in the form of Italian opera. But before the Reformation and for a time after, all England sang. All the Elizabethan dramatists break into the lyrical strain, with more or less success, according to the fineness of their feeling and their ear. John Addington Symonds[1] says that the lyrical element "pervaded all species of poetry in the Elizabethan age. . . . We then had a native school of composers, and needed not to know the melodies of other lands. Every house had its lute suspended on the parlor wall. In every company of men and women part-songs were sung." Shakespeare, the foremost expresser of his time, was the most lyrical, the most songful, of all its writers. Dramatic expression may be full and noble without the musical cadence accentuated, — without that extravagance of figures, that play of the fancy, that redundance of imaginative suggestion, that lark-like flight which is sustained lyricism. There are many such forms of noble dramatic expression in Shakespeare.

[1] The Lyrism of the English Romantic Drama. A Paper written for the Elizabethan Society of Toynbee Hall.

The great scene between Hamlet and his mother is not lyrical, though it has the measured movement of metrical cadences. It does not suggest the chant, though it is intense to the finest degree. A drama may be lyrical in the noblest sense; an ode must be lyrical in the noblest sense, though in our time we have lost sight of the real meaning of lyrical and almost limited it to sweet songs of the type of which Tennyson gives us perfect specimens in "The Princess."

It would be unnecessary to show that lyrism was one of the principal qualities of the Greek drama, and that, as Newman says, it was founded on no scientific principle; "it was a pure recreation of the imagination, revelling without object or meaning beyond its own exhibition."[1] The belief that holds that there is a wide gulf between the classicism of Sophocles and the romantic lyrism of Shakespeare is unfounded. They were more akin than most of us imagine. While Racine and Corneille are nearer to Aristotle than Shakespeare, Shakespeare

[1] Poetry with Reference to Aristotle's Poetics.

is nearer to Sophocles and Euripides than Racine and Corneille. The presence of the declamatory, the eloquent quality, is evident in the French tragedians, but seldom does the lyrical quality appear. There is always reticence, the restraint of feeling modulated by rigid rule, seldom the imaginative, emotional outburst, put there by the author without regard to the action of the drama, and never the little song so metred that its every accent and pause suggest the combination of notes by which the composer will make it ready for his harp. When poetical expression is over-abundant and conveys the impression that it might be chanted, or sung, or even read to musical accompaniment, it is lyrical. Hamlet's

> Confess yourself to Heaven;
> Repent what's past: avoid what is to come,

is not a lyrical cry; nor is the Queen's outburst,

> O Hamlet, thou hast cleft my heart in twain.

But there is lyricism — so overstrained that it nearly becomes bombastic rhetoric

—in the dialogue between Hamlet and Laertes at the grave of Ophelia, in the Queen's description of Ophelia's death, and in speech after speech in Richard II. For instance (Act III, Scene 2):

> Dear earth, I do salute thee with my hand,
> Though rebels wound thee with their horses' hoofs;
> As a long-parted mother with her child
> Plays fondly with her tears and smiles in meeting,
> So, weeping, smiling, greet I thee, my earth,
> And do thee favours with my royal hands.

If Molière's "L'Avare" and Goldsmith's "She Stoops to Conquer" are comedies, Shakespeare's "As You Like It," "A Midsummer Night's Dream," "The Tempest," and "The Winter's Tale" certainly are not; and "Love's Labour's Lost" and "Twelfth Night" —in fact, all except "The Comedy of Errors" and "The Taming of the Shrew" are very defective ones. Dialogue and dramatic interest and action, realism, constitute a comedy. How extravagant, how impossible, how undramatic, how exquisitely lyrical in every sense is "As You Like It"! As for the characters which have any hold on local reality, they are Elizabethans, though they live in No Man's Land. In essence, all except Oliver are universal. Music is everywhere in the atmosphere of the play. There are intervals of prose, like the expository conversation between Adam and Orlando, in the first act, and all the speeches until the shadow of the tyrant Duke falls upon the scene. There are hints of music, as if the violinists were trying their instruments, but the lyrical quality of the play is not shown until we enter the Forest of Arden. The sentiment of the forest permeates every line until Amiens begins to sing:

> Under the greenwood tree
> Who loves to lie with me,
> And turn his merry note
> Unto the sweet bird's throat,
> Come hither, come hither, come hither;
> Here shall he see
> No enemy
> But Winter and rough weather.

Then comes the chorus:

> Who doth ambition shun,
> And loves to live i' the sun,
> Seeking the food he eats,
> And pleased with what he gets,

> Come hither, come hither, come hither;
>   Here shall he see
>   No enemy
> But Winter and rough weather.

There are many passages where the overwrought, high-strained appeal to the imagination seems to resemble the euphuistic affectation which Shakespeare ridiculed in Polonius and Osric,—the speeches at the grave in "Hamlet" are examples. In extenuation, it must be remembered that the theatre of Shakespeare was barren of all those accessories which force stage effects upon our sight to-day. There were no waving leaves, where shadows are cast by calcium lights upon tufts of grass, in the Globe or the Rose Theatre, at the end of the sixteenth century. At court the Queen's Master of the Revels, Edmund Tylney, could command scenic apparatus almost as splendid as Calderon used at the Palace of Buen Retiro. But the theatre of Shakespeare, where the royal masques were not given, was forced to appeal through the ear rather than the eye.

A boy acted Rosalind or Ophelia, Perdita or Juliet, and the fairies in "A

Midsummer Night's Dream" were rosy-cheeked urchins, more suggestive of roast beef and Yorkshire pudding than moonlight and cobwebs. Most of us more enjoy a play of Shakespeare's read in quietness than presented to us subject to all the accidents of theatrical realism. This is because Shakespeare left nothing to such accidents. With no scenery and sometimes not even a screen, the sides of his platform occupied by loungers, without the means of changing the effect from light to darkness, he is obliged to force the illusion by the imaginative powers of the text. He cannot keep the expressions of his characters down to the level of ordinary life; their speech must soar in imagination and it must have in expression musical cadences. The modern opera has its reason in this need to be lyrical. It is artificial; it can never, if it retain its absurd *libretti* or depend on the Wagnerian effects, appeal to the imagination as cadenced lyrical dramas, such as "As You Like It" and "The Tempest"; for the imagination is clogged, held down, by too much realism. The desire to uplift by means of sonorous lyrical words set to music is at the root of the creation of the opera. The Church — if I may be permitted to say so — has, especially in the Tenebræ, shown how far dramatic suggestiveness may go without dragging the imagination too near reality. Shakespeare was an unconscious psychologist, and he, applying his genius to lesser themes, understood admirably the essential quality of suggestion. When rhetoric seems, as with Laertes, to approach rant, it is the result of the poet's determination to make the lounging gallants and the citizens and 'prentice boys forget themselves in the high-pitched passion of the moment, — for this great artist could rely only on the influence of uttered words. His soliloquies — dramatic expediency forcing him to make his character speak to the public the very processes of his secret thought — are unquestioned by men of taste, because their seriousness and dignity are supported by fitting musical cadences. Under the master's art-spell, we forget that the sable-hued Hamlet ought to be absurd as he stands — the other characters having conveniently left him alone — not in self-communing silence, but in outspoken analysis of his own mind. Shakespeare meant to bear our imaginations into his world, and he succeeded; he is more of a magician than Prospero.

Perhaps of all the plays, "As You Like It" is most lyrical in structure. Newman says:

> "We may liken the Greek drama to the music of the Italian school; in which the wonder is, how so much richness of invention in detail can be accommodated to a style so simple and uniform. Each is the development of grace, fancy, pathos, and taste, in the respective media of representation and sound."

Dr. Newman may have thought of the school of Mozart, but certainly not of the artificialities of Donizetti or Bellini. Similarly, "As You Like It" resembles the structure which underlies the operas of the Italian composers. There are recitatives, the duets, arias, and those particularly English madrigal effects, which accentuate the pastoral feeling when the imagination needs the stimulus of more pronounced music. The Duke opens the first scene in the forest with the *recitativo* which closes:

> Sweet are the uses of adversity,
> Which, like the toad, ugly and venomous,
> Wears yet a precious jewel in his head; [1]
> And this our life exempt from public haunt
> Finds tongues in trees, books in the running brooks,
> Sermons in stones, and good in everything.
> I would not change it.

There is a snatch of dialogue between the exiled Duke and Amiens, and the First Lord begins his *recitativo*, — and an exquisitely lyrical one it is, — the description of the oak and the deer, and the moralizing of the melancholy Jaques. It impedes the action; Molière would not have tolerated it; modern theatrical managers cut it out; it would be permitted only in a musical play.

The lyrical phrases change and interweave. Silvius breaks forth:

> O, thou did'st then ne'er love so heartily!
> If thou remember'st not the slightest folly
> That ever love did make thee run into,
> Thou hast not loved;
> Or if thou hast not sat as I do now,
> Wearying thy hearer in thy mistress' praise,
> Thou hast not loved;
> Or if thou hast not broke from company
> Abruptly, as my passion now makes me,
> Thou hast not loved.

When Orlando appeals to the foresters for his fainting old servant, Adam, we hear the same cadences, artfully changed, —

> But whate'er you are
> That in this desert inaccessible,
> Under the shade of melancholy boughs,
> Lose and neglect the creeping hours of time;
> If ever you have look'd on better days,
> If ever been where bells have knoll'd to church,
> If ever sat at any good man's feast,
> If ever from your eyelids wiped a tear
> And know what 't is to pity and be pitied,
> Let gentleness my strong enforcement be;
> In the which hope I blush, and hide my sword.

And when Jaques has ended his sad *recitativo*,

> All the world's a stage,

Shakespeare waves his baton, and the meditative mood is relieved, but not interrupted by the lusty Amiens:

> Blow, blow, thou winter wind,
> Thou art not so unkind
>   As man's ingratitude;
> Thy tooth is not so keen,
> Because thou art not seen,
>   Although thy breath be rude.

With a rush the chorus comes in —

Heigh-ho, sing heigh-ho! unto the green holly:
Most friendship is feigning, most loving mere folly:
    Then, heigh-ho, the holly!
    This life is most jolly.

Amiens regains the thread of the melody:

> Freeze, freeze, thou bitter sky,
> That dost not bite so nigh
>   As benefits forgot:
> Though thou the waters warp,
> Thy sting is not so sharp
>   As friend remember'd not.

Orlando opens Scene 2 of Act III with a new rhymed lyrical movement, and disappears to let the inferior Corin and Touchstone talk in everyday prose. In Scene 2 of Act V there is the quartette of Silvius, Phebe, Rosalind, and Orlando, with the suggestion of the fugue. It is not set to the music of the composer, and there is no direction in the text for musical accompaniment, but no reader could utter it without making verbal music the recurrent cadence:

Phe. Good shepherd, tell this youth what 't is to love.
Sil. It is to be all made of sighs and tears;
And so am I for Phebe.

Phe. And I for Ganymede.
Orl. And I for Rosalind.
Ros. And I for no woman.

Silvius has his solo part:

It is to be all made of fantasy,
All made of passion, and all made of wishes,
All adoration, duty, and observance,
All humbleness, all patience and impatience,
All purity, all trial, all observance,
And so am I for Phebe.
Phe. And so am I for Ganymede.
Orl. And so am I for Rosalind.
Ros. And so am I for no woman.

Phebe, after this cadence, takes a new rhythmical modulation —

Phe. If this be so, why blame you me to love you?
Sil. If this be so, why blame you me to love you?
Orl. If this be so, why blame you me to love you?
Ros. Who do you speak to, "Why blame you me to love you?"
Orl. To her that is not here, nor doth not hear.

The last act is made up of musical cadences, with a short interval of prose. The vocal fugue is imitated, especially in the speeches of Jaques and Rosalind, and the real song of that act is Hymen's:

> Then is there mirth in heaven
> When earthly things made even
>   Atone together.

"The Winter's Tale" is lyrical from beginning to end. The rogue, Autolycus, has some delightful snatches of song:

> When daffodils begin to peer

and

> Lawn as white as driven snow;
> Cyprus black as e'er was crow;
> Gloves as sweet as damask roses;
> Masks for faces and for noses.

And his part in the trio with Dorcas and Mopsa —

> Get you hence, for I must go,
> Where it fits not you to know.
>   *D.* Whither? *M.* Oh, whither? *D.* Whither?

For the delicate management of the pauses, for musical suggestiveness, for convincing appeal to the fancy, what can be better than the trio of the Shepherd, Polixenes, and Perdita, in Act IV, Scene 4:

>   O Proserpina,
> For the flowers now, that, frighted, thou let'st fall
> From Dis's waggon! daffodils,
> That come before the swallow dares, and take

The winds of March with beauty; violets dim,
But sweeter than the lids of Juno's eyes
Or Cytherea's breath.

There is the aubade, in "Cymbeline," which bursts through the prose of Cloten's speech:

> Hark, hark! the lark at heaven's gate sings,
>   And Phœbus 'gins arise,
> His steeds to water at those springs
>   On chaliced flowers that lies;
> And winking Mary-buds begin
>   To ope their golden eyes:
> With everything that pretty is,
>   My lady sweet, arise,
>   Arise, arise!

Over Imogen's body Arviragus speaks:

We'll say our song the whilst. Brother, begin.

Gui. Fear no more the heat o' the sun,
    Nor the furious winter's rages;
  Thou thy worldly task hast done,
    Home art gone, and ta'en thy wages;
  Golden lads and girls all must
  As chimney-sweepers, come to dust.

Arv. Fear no more the frown o' the great;
    Thou art past the tyrant's stroke;
  Care no more to clothe and eat;
    To thee the reed is as the oak;
  The sceptre, learning, physic, must
  All follow this, and come to dust.

Gui. Fear no more the lightning-flash,
Arv.   Nor the all-dreaded thunder-stone.
Gui. Fear not slander, censure rash;
Arv.   Thou hast finished joy and moan.
Both. All lovers young, all lovers must
Consign to thee, and come to dust.

Gui. No exorciser harm thee!
Arv. Nor no witchcraft charm thee!
Gui. Ghost unlaid forbear thee!
Arv. Nothing ill come near thee!
Both. Quiet consummation have,
And renowned be thy grave!

Mr. Symonds says:

" These songs cannot be regarded as occasional ditties, interpolated for the delectation of the audience. . . . They condense the particular emotion of the tragedy or comedy in a quintessential drop of melody. Mr. Pater has dwelt upon a single instance of this fact with his usual felicity of phrase. Speaking of the song in 'Measure for Measure,' he remarks that in it the kindling power and poetry of the whole play seem to pass for a moment into an actual strain of music."

It *is* an actual strain of music, needing neither string nor wind instrument, but only the inspiration of unforced breath. It has all the qualities of music except pitch.

Portia was musical. When it comes to

Bassanio's turn to choose the casket, she is devoured with anxiety. She cannot tell him that the leaden box contains the key of his fate and hers. He, led by deluding fancy, may choose the gold or silver box. She must not speak, she cannot give him a hint in words of hers, but another may sing. She confesses this to nobody, but makes a prelude to her carefully chosen lyric:

> Let music sound while he doth make his choice;
> Then, if he lose, he makes a swan-like end,
> Fading in music.

And, while Bassanio comments on the caskets to himself, the song goes on:

> Tell me where is fancy bred,
> Or in the heart or in the head?
> How begot, how nourished?
>   Reply, reply.
> It is engender'd in the eyes,
> With gazing fed; and fancy dies
> In the cradle where it lies.
>   Let us all ring fancy's knell;
>   I'll begin it — Ding, dong, bell.
> *All.* Ding, dong, bell.

Bassanio had more than the usual vanity of his sex, and he was as thoughtlessly selfish as any other spirited gallant of his time, but he had a pretty wit and he catches the hint.

> So may the outward shows be least themselves;
> The world is still deceived with ornament.

On the message of this lyric depends the turn of the play, and yet how easily and naturally it is dropped in! It falls so gently that it seems to be a gliding strain caught as a point of rest in the suspensive interest of the moment, but it determines Bassanio's action.

There are musicians who thank heaven for "A Midsummer Night's Dream" because it suggested Mendelssohn's music. Herr Ambros, in "The Boundaries of Music and Poetry," seems to draw very near to this. He says:

> "When we are listening to the wonderfully elusive, fluttering, skipping, bantering G-minor *scherzo* (this miracle of instrumentation) introducing Puck's roguish pranks, we believe everything which the poet relates of him — before our eyes, Puck skips into the side scenes; to our ears, he actually flies like the arrow from the Indian's bow; and we believe the ear more than the eye."

This is true — but only after we have known the play and steeped ourselves in the scent of the musk-roses and seen the moonlight on the banks of wild thyme. It is to the ear that Shakespeare speaks, — even a cursory study of his lyrism will make that plain; he speaks through music, but it is a music more evanescent, less palpable, but more directly expressive than Mendelssohn's, because it is a music essential to the words themselves, not a set of musical sounds speaking a composer's impressions of them. Where Shakespeare has given

> To airy nothing
> A local habitation and a name,

Mendelssohn interprets it in music; the G-minor scherzo might mean almost anything gay, if the composer of "Songs without Words" had not told us of the theme on which he founded it. No; the music of Mendelssohn may suggest, but never so directly and unequivocally as the metred phrases of the lyrist. Shakespeare knew this, and, better than this, he knew that his appeal must be by concordant words to the emotions, through the imagination.

He must make pictures too. And in the old days at Stratford, in the homely country lanes and fields, he had gathered all the material for these pictures. The folk-song heard at twilight, the glimpse of the spot in the chalice of the cowslip like a drop of blood, the dying fall of the madrigal as the shepherds went their way to the shearing, the daisies "smell-less, yet most quaint," — all these had become part of his younger life, and about them sounded the echoes of the glees and rustic dances. Thus the picture and the accented words were one.

No realism can altogether ruin the lyrism of "A Midsummer Night's Dream"; for the poet, forced to soar above the sordid surroundings of his theatre, made an appeal with all the strength of his genius, strengthened by many garnered treasures drawn from Nature herself, which Mendelssohn or Berlioz could only suggest, but never reach. The pleasanter dramas of Shakespeare, without the lyrism, would still be the masterpieces of character and philosophy taken from life, but they would not deserve the name of comedies in Molière's sense, nor could they be justly held to compare with his. They would lack that exquisite, permeative charm that makes them the most beautiful things of their kind under heaven. And the strength of this charm is in part due to the fact that even the smallest lyric arises from the feeling of the composition and intensifies it. The melodious "Spring Song" at the end of "Love's Labor's Lost" is at once a conclusion and a harbinger. Mendelssohn, the composer, recalls the Spring, but only when we know beforehand that he intends to recall it; the "Winter Song" has the meaning of an epilogue. And the very bloom of the mood of the Duke, in "Twelfth Night," is accented by

> That old and antique song we heard last night:
> Methought it did relieve my passion much,
> More than light airs and recollected terms
> Of these most brisk and giddy-paced times:
> Come, but one verse. . . .

> "Come away, come away, death,
>   And in sad cypress let me be laid."

And the Prince Ferdinand's amazement is turned to sad remembrance by Ariel's song, which is as much a part of the feeling of the moment as the glow is in a ruby.

> Full fathom five thy father lies;
>   Of his bones are coral made;
> Those are pearls that were his eyes;
> Nothing of him that doth fade
>   But doth suffer a sea-change
> Into something rich and strange.
> Sea-nymphs hourly ring his knell:
>   Ding-dong.
> Hark! now I hear them, — Ding-dong, bell.

What can be said of these lyrics, except that, whether invented by Shakespeare or borrowed from antique songs, they were made by him essential to the works in which they appear? While their echoes are with me I shall write no more; for, as Armado says,

> The words of Mercury are harsh after the songs
> Of Apollo. You that way; we this way.

THE PUZZLE OF HAMLET

THE PUZZLE OF HAMLET

"THE puzzle of Hamlet" is a phrase frequently repeated; and the more "Hamlet" is considered by the critics, the oftener it is repeated. The reasons for it may be found in the lack of serious study given to the text of this incomparable drama and psychological study, as well as in the neglect by readers of culture of the contemporary literature of Shakespeare's time. Added to these is the strange habit of guessing at Shakespeare's meaning from a modern point of view. This habit is fixed by the determination of so many persons to read the past as if we possessed the one ray capable of illuminating it. It is as if we thought the secrets of old rolls of papyrus could reveal themselves only under the rays of the electric light. "Hamlet" has been made a puzzle because of our inability to look at the text from the point of view of a contemporary. "'Ow could Shakespeare 'ave lived in such a nasty 'ouse without gas?" asked a Cockney at Stratford. It is easy to supply the gas.

In one of the most scholarly works in the department of English literature written in the last fifteen years, "A History of Criticism," George Saintsbury says, speaking of the critical necessity of confining ourselves to the actual texts:

"This is not perhaps a fashionable proceeding. Not what Plato says, but what the latest commentator says about Plato; not what Chaucer says, but what the latest thesis-writer thinks about Chaucer, — is supposed to be the qualifying study of the scholar. I am not able to share this conception of scholarship. When we have read and digested the whole of Plato, we may, if we like, turn to his latest German editor; when we have read and digested the whole of Shakespeare, and of Shakespeare's contemporaries, we may, if we like, turn to Shakespearean biographers and commentators."

A fault in much Shakespearean criticism is that it is too reverential. The writer who scans the Bible, alert to find an anachronism or an exaggeration, sprawls at full length before the silliest "sallet" of the Bard of Avon, or perhaps of Messrs. Hemynge and Condell, in rapt admiration. Hysterical girls after a morning recital by Paderewski are no more ecstatic than some of the Shakespearean acolytes. This blazon ought not to be; it makes Shakespeare an idol hidden in clouds of incense, an idol to be worshipped as unreasoningly as all idols are worshipped. From what we can discover of the English of the sixteenth century — and no great list of historical references is needed to show this — we know that they regarded a play as a play, not as an enigma to be thought about, written about, discussed as a problem in philosophy. All the reconstructions of the Elizabethan playhouse show that the auditors went there to weep or laugh, to love the hero and to detest the villain, to applaud the good and to hate the bad. The recent revival of the Catholic morality play, "Everyman," ought to give us a clue to the truth that the drama in England, from the day of its appearance in the monasteries to the day of its disappearance under the ban of ultra-Protestantism, was written to be seen and heard, not to be read or academically analyzed. Again, although we talk of the continuity of history, we do not take seriously the truth it implies,—that in essentials human nature has always been the same, and that by recognizing these essentials we get the keys to many things of the past that are closed to us by the unconscious assumption that we are a new order of beings, transformed by the Reformation and experimental philosophy!

That the Elizabethans and the Jacobeans did not, in the space of a few years, break completely with the beliefs and traditions of the Roman Catholic Church; that they, in spite of the manner in which distance and romance have transfigured them, took a matter-of-fact view of life; and that there were varying shades of belief, opinion, and taste are facts that might well be taken into consideration in discussing the meaning of "Hamlet." No audience will flock to a playhouse to see a tragedy which it does not understand or with which it is out of sympathy. The moralities and miracle plays were almost too obvious for our present taste, but not more than sufficiently obvious for the liking of the English of the fifteenth and sixteenth centuries. The dramas of Shakespeare, Fletcher, Chapman, and the rest may contain a cipher: that is another question. It is certain that the noble earl who liked to listen to music or to mingle with his countrymen of a lower caste at bear-baitings did not go to see "Hamlet" for the zest of solving any problem, whether in cipher or not.

A lover of Shakespeare, recognizing these things, has two quarrels on his hands, or, at least, two reasons for irritation in his mind. One is with the expositor of "Hamlet" who treats the text as a mere matter for the student; the other with the actor who, having in his art so many means that make for clarity, uses the play as if his own personality were the first thought, and the meaning of the author the second. To these reasons for discontent may be added the student's disregard of the actor's part in the making of the play, and the actor's slavish obedience, in minor details, to the student. The student forgets that "Hamlet" was written to be acted, and the actor does not recognize that neither philological guesses of the note-maker nor the exact shape of Laertes' cloak is of consequence, provided the value of each character be so expressed that the meaning of the tragedy is full and clear. When the actor can impress on the student that, if "intuitional" interpretation is to be allowed, he has the advantage, because he is forced in the exercise of his art to take Shakespeare's point of view, we may have less critical dust thrown in our eyes.

There is now no difference of opinion as to the position of "Hamlet" in the literature of the world, Voltaire having been long ago thrown out of court. Insight into man's heart and mind, and into the fundamental varieties which underlie life, expressed in words of piercing beauty and aptness, is acknowledged to exist in this play to an amazing degree; but if the art form in which these appear is defective, the symmetry of the masterpiece is affected. In a word, if the play does not answer all the requirements of a play, if it is not interesting and clear, Shakespeare made a serious mistake in adopting the dramatic form. If Shakespeare was not sure whether Hamlet was mad or not, or whether he was noble or not, or whether he loved Ophelia or not, or whether Gertrude had sinned or not, he had the commentators of the future in his mind's eye, and he wrote for them; but as his utter disregard of the future of his written plays shows that he did not consider the commentators, he must have had in mind an immediate audience. And for the audience of the moment the dramatist must be sure of what he wants to say, and must say it with vigor. There have been exceptions, no doubt, but not enough to prove that a so-called drama, of the vagueness of one of Henry James's novels, could hold the attention of normal auditors. From the first, "Hamlet," as a play, is clear and admirably constructed to meet the demands of the London stage of the time.

A glance at the source of the play — the "Historie of Hamblet" — connotes the evident purpose of Shakespeare to show that the Prince of Denmark counterfeits madness. Hamblet, in the "Historie," is, however, a very young prince, who imitates Brutus, because he knows that his father-uncle, Fengon, suspects that he will avenge his father's murder as soon as he comes of age. He is a pagan, and he thinks and acts as a pagan; but Shakespeare was too much of his own time to be able to project himself into a pagan mind, and too much of an artist to forgo the opportunities offered by a conflict between Christianity and that nature which Edmund in his famous soliloquy called his "goddess." In this conflict lies the pregnant interest of the play.

If Hamlet had Edmund's contempt for any law but nature's, the play would have lost its deep dramatic interest. In the "Historie of Hamblet," as in Malory's "Morte Arthure," paganism shows plainly through the Christian veneering. The translators apologize for this, conscious always of the lack of sympathy in their readers for a prince, no matter how greatly injured, who would thirst for the mere satisfaction of vengeance. In "Hamlet" the pagan man bursts through the habits of the Christian mind. The young Prince will not kill Claudius at his prayers:

> Now might I do it pat, now he is praying ;
> And now I 'll do 't. And so he goes to heaven ;
> And so am I revenged. That would be scann'd :
> A villain kills my father ; and for that,
> I, his sole son, do this same villain send
> To heaven.
> O, this is hire and salary, not revenge.

The pagan writing on the palimpsest has not been entirely effaced. Whether Shakespeare had read the " Historie of Hamblet " or not, or whether he founded " Hamlet " on an old tragedy derived from the " Historie," it is evident that he had at least at heart the conflict between Christian law and that lawlessness, that giving way to natural impulses, — to desire or hatred, knowing no law, — which we call pagan. How coolly, too, Hamlet sends his treacherous friends, Rosencrantz and Guildenstern, to their death ! His excuse would have seemed a valid one to Elizabethans, for the traitorous friends had been privy to a plot for compassing the ruin of one of the royal blood, and the rightful heir to the throne. Horatio is astonished that these two fellow-students should be let go straight to their fate. Hamlet says :

> Why, man, they did make love to this employment;
> They are not near my conscience; their defeat
> Does by their own insinuation grow.

Hamlet does not doom these traitors to death in madness; it is not madness that makes him spare the King's life until he can think that the murder will plunge him into hell. He is frenzied for the moment, when he kills Polonius, behind the arras, believing that Claudius is listening there; he is nervously overwrought, and in the overwhelming horror of the Ghost's revelation, striving for self-control, until, in the tumult of heart and brain, he seems unbalanced and hysterical, but never, even for a moment, mad. The madness that he alludes to, in his pathetic words to Laertes, is evidenced in those episodes. It is the loss of that habitual balance which he admires so much in Horatio, who is never "passion's slave." Passion's slave at times Hamlet is. In this consists his madness.

Hamlet is essentially noble; he may decline from the law, but he knows, loves, and respects it. Claudius, on the other hand, being a man of parts, knows and hates it; he sins, and trembles before God, but before man he is every inch a king, in spite of Hamlet's passionate exaggeration of his defects. He accepts evil with open eyes. He would be virtuous if virtue could be reconciled with friendship for the world, the flesh, and the devil. He would be good if he were not compelled to make satisfaction for evil done to his neighbor. Luther's comfortable doctrine about works had not been preached in Shakespeare's Denmark. Claudius is no mere "king of shreds and patches," though some of the commentators and most of the actors make him so, — as they make an arrant fool or a comic knave of Polonius, who was an accomplished Euphuist and a clever courtier.

It is impossible to enjoy the play, as a clear and logical work, without keeping in mind that it was written for the theatre, acted under the direction of Shakespeare, and made actual by what the stage-manager in our time would call "business." And this "business," — the technical direction for the dumb show, or the actions suited to the word,

— which elucidates the meaning of speech, must have been as delicately and carefully considered as is every line in the text. The record of this "business" we have lost, and the loss is irreparable. If it existed, the student who looks on "Hamlet" as a text detached from dramatic action would not have had matters so much his own way, and the actor who derives most of his traditions from the practice of other actors of no greater knowledge than himself would not cause intelligent lovers of Shakespeare to wish that "Hamlet" might never be degraded by the glare of the footlights. Nevertheless, the impulse of the actor to cause the play to be as obvious as possible has wrought good results. The actor knows, what our critics do not seem always to know, that no accomplished playwright wants to obscure the processes or the objects of his drama, or to convert an acting play into an elusive study as Orphic as one of Richard Strauss's symphonic poems. He may, and he generally does, neglect every other character in the play, to round out that of the Prince; but at his worst he must regard the action as well as the words. His consciousness of an audience that does not care to think forces him to present effectively what the student in his closet refines, re-refines, and over-refines. Hamlet, with him, is a man, not a mind divorced from a man, and he has not such a superstitious regard for the text that he will allow words to stand, merely as words which have no meaning, if not illumined by gesture or facial expression. The actor makes mistakes at times: in his passion for effects, he overleaps truth, as when, after the death of Polonius, he weeps and groans in most unprincely fashion. Hamlet says:

> For this same lord
> I do repent: but heaven hath pleased it so,
> To punish me with this and this with me,
> That I must be their scourge and minister.

At the end of this most dramatic scene Hamlet "drags in the body of Polonius,"[1] the Queen hurrying away by another door. The actor who should coolly and cruelly obey the stage direction would bring upon himself the hisses of

---

[1] "Exeunt severally; Hamlet dragging in the body of Polonius."

the auditors and destroy all sympathy for Hamlet, unless it is presumed that he had suddenly become insane. The text of the interview between Hamlet and his mother ought to render that supposition out of the question, although Gertrude, horrified by the effect of the Ghost's appearance on her son, says:

> This is the very coinage of your brain:
> This bodiless creation ecstasy
> Is very cunning in.

She does not see her husband, Hamlet's father, "in his habit as he lived," come to hold the Prince, by the bonds of love, to his "almost blunted purpose." "Taint not thy mind," the spirit of the King — suffering, unpurged of crimes, not great in the eyes of men, but foul before the purity of God — has said. And now, not as a king, not as an outraged patriot seeing with clear eyes that sin is corrupting Denmark, and that the roots of the cancer must be torn out by Hamlet, but as a suppliant for the soul of the Queen, he comes. That the "illusion" was no illusion in the modern sense is shown by the stage direction in the First Folio,

"Enter the Ghost." That the Ghost was no hallucination in the beginning of the play, Shakespeare takes pains to prove by the testimony of the soldiers, and, more convincing than all, by the evidence of the clear-minded Horatio. As Hamlet was not mad, the dragging in of Polonius could not have been the only business set down for Hamlet after the exit of his mother; and "severally" is not sufficiently definite.

The actor whose instinct is true sees this, and supplies the business to save the situation. At times he is intemperate, — there have been actors who grovelled at the feet of Polonius and howled with grief in the most unprincely manner and unphilosophical fashion. The student does not, as a rule, weep at all or conceive that Hamlet could have wept. He takes the text as it stands, and Hamlet, instead of for the moment assuming a coldness that he does not feel to impress the Queen with the surety of his purpose, becomes brutal in madness. Much of the text of Shakespeare, which seems inconsistent and is therefore held to have deep and even occult meaning by isolated students, simply needs the theatrical business — not set down in the stage Folio or the Quarto — to be clear and consistent. In minor passages this is very plain. For instance, in the First Act, when the Ghost passes, and Horatio cries out, —

> I'll cross it, though it blast me,

the business explanatory of this is differently interpreted by actors, and though great play is made with the cross-handles of the swords in the swearing scene, the usual method is for Horatio merely to cross the path of the Ghost. The famous romantic player, Fechter, made the sign of the cross, and, as the Ghost did not flinch, — as it would have done had it been an evil spirit, — he went on with his truly Christian appeal to a spirit in a process of purgation:

> If there be any good thing to be done,
> That may to thee do ease and grace to me,
> Speak to me:
> If thou art privy to thy country's fate,
> Which, happily, foreknowing may avoid,
> O, speak!

What the actor of the Ghost did in Shakespeare's time, we have no means of knowing. The business accompanying Hamlet's

> Look here, upon this picture, and on this,

is not even so important, yet it is sometimes a piece of very gross exaggeration. It will never be possible for an actor to insert the business in the grave-diggers' scene, as described by M. de la Baume Desdossat, when he said that the author "fait jouer à la boule avec des têtes de mort sur le théâtre." The bowling with death's heads on the stage might easily be introduced to exemplify Hamlet's allusion to the old game of "loggats" by the performers who wanted to accentuate the Gothic and grim humor of the clowns. Knight smiles at the statement of the exquisite M. Desdossat, and yet some of the business introduced by the theatrical gravediggers is not less grotesque; and who can conclude that it is really out of keeping in the awful contrast Shakespeare makes? There is, as I have said, the evidence of no prompters' books to the contrary. The taste of the time is the only limit one can set to the grotesque in Shakespeare or in any author of his period. It is evident from the text that the spirit of Shakespeare is against exaggeration of any kind, and the taste of our time is with his. The actor of to-day runs a great risk when, as Laertes, he stands over the body of Ophelia, saturated with the water of the pool and bound by clinging plants, and says:

> Too much of water hast thou, poor Ophelia,
> And therefore I forbid my tears: but yet
> It is our trick; nature her custom holds,
> Let shame say what it will: when these are gone,
> The woman will be out.

Often these lines are omitted, and with reason. The actor is on delicate ground in uttering what, in our time, seems a bombastic exaggeration. We cannot tell whether Shakespeare softened his rhetoric by business. At any rate, we can be sure that the lines were delivered under Shakespeare's direction, so that they could in no way interfere with the pathos of the moment. The modesty of nature seems to be outraged by them, as they stand in cold print; but who can say that, from the actor's point of view,—which was also Shakespeare's,—they were not so presented that even to-day they would not have offended our taste? In most of our modern plays every direction is carefully written ; no doubt is left by the author in the mind of the reader as to the exact position of any character at any given time on the stage. But these minute directions do not appear in the reading edition of the play, — though, as a rule, the literary quality of modern plays is so poor that nobody cares to read them. They are arranged for the stage, and when they disappear from the stage, their value likewise disappears. They exist, like the score of an opera by Verdi, or a symphony of Beethoven, only when they are interpreted.

Shakespeare's meaning suffers when his plays are read as if they were intended merely to be read. A poet of the first class, and, consequently, a transfigurer of life, an interpreter of the fundamentals and universals of human character, he chose the form of expression most adapted to the feeling and taste of his time. It has been noticed many times that the limitations of the Elizabethan playhouse forced him to adopt a method more akin to that of the modern novelist than that of the modern playwright. His characters tell us, in their speeches, many things of local and temporal import which, in the modern play, are indicated, through the change in the theatrical apparatus, to the sight. The Queen's description of the death of Ophelia, and the poetic expression of Jacques's reveries would be mere "words, words, words," to the theatrical writer of the present day, who uses words in order to make pictures as seldom as possible. When Gower enters, at the beginning of the fifth act of "Pericles," he asks the auditors to do what the novelist often asks his readers to do, — to "make believe," to "suppose."

> In your supposing once more put your sight
> Of heavy Pericles; think this his bark:
> Where what is done in action, more, if might,
> Shall be discover'd; please you, sit and hark.

The audience of to-day neither "supposes" nor "sits and harks." It sits and sees. Shakespeare could not adapt his plays to the modern theatre without destroying their literary value. At the same time they would have lost their power of appeal to the folk of his time, were they literature only, and not dumb show, at times, and very vigorous action as well.

The characters of Regan and Goneril in "King Lear" seem to be monsters of evil without any attractive traits. They are so wicked that many lovers of Shakespeare have classed them as theatrical puppets created as foils to Cordelia. And it must be confessed that the bare text gives this impression, for there are few phrases concerning them that suggest to the imagination that they are more than twin creatures wedded, unhumanly, to sin. Edmund, too, seems unhuman, — a mind of lust and lawlessness, a pawn of the author's to bring out one of the emphatic lessons of the play, that sin blinds us to the truth, — that both Lear and Gloucester suffered because, wedded to their pet sins, their minds had grown so darkened that they could not distinguish truth from falsehood. But neither Regan nor Goneril is a mere puppet. Regan and Goneril differ in attributes. Albany calls Goneril "a gilded serpent"; and on this hint the actor should build.

Goneril and Regan are too often treated as evil twins, in no way different except in their love for Edmund. As for Edmund, he is most dependent on the actor; the text is full of subtle hints, not always considered by either the reader or the personator. Edgar says:

> The gods are just, and of our pleasant vices
> Make instruments to plague us:
> The dark and vicious place where thee he got
> Cost him his eyes.

And Edmund replies:

> Thou hast spoken right, 't is true;
> The wheel is come full circle; I am here.

Dying, Edmund goes back, in triumph, to his sin again:

> Yet Edmund was beloved:
> The one the other poison'd for my sake,
> And after slew herself.

Edmund is a character created for the actor, and it requires all the art of artful actors to interpret his subtlety. The puzzle-questions as to Edmund — Is he an atheist? Is he not a mere creature of circumstances? — become quite plain when Edmund appears in flesh and blood, with a will to choose Nature as his goddess, and a belief, at least, in nature's law. Iago himself, a self-degraded and super-subtle soul, is, too, human only in the actor's hands. His plottings, read in cold blood, on the printed page, make him seem to be simply a devil, sojourning for a time on earth in human form.

On the other hand, the theatre has a way of being careful in minor details, which are often stifling to the imagination, and careless in more important things not considered in a certain class of modern novels. A manager who prides himself on the minutiæ of a gondola in "The Merchant of Venice" or on the fidelity to detail in the view of a Venetian street in "Othello" will cut out those most important lines in the speech of the Ghost in "Hamlet," —

> Unhousel'd, disappointed, unaneled.

They seem unimportant to the reader of Shakespeare who cannot conceive — being without present knowledge of historical data — their terrible meaning:

> Unhousel'd, disappointed, unaneled,
> No reckoning made, but sent to my account
> With all my imperfections on my head:
> O, horrible! O, horrible! most horrible!

The spirit's heart-wrung exclamation is that he died without the last sacraments, disappointed of his rights as a Christian, unshriven, without extreme unction. The statement affects Hamlet terribly; we learn it later in the play. Hamlet broods on it, and he does not keep in mind that the Ghost is not a lost soul, though suffering the pains of purgation; that he thinks only of those pains we know well from his soliloquy over the praying Claudius. Less archæology and more art, less attention to the conditions of minds in the play, would do away with the aspersion that the theatre, in the United States at least, has no historical sense.

The accent laid by the spirit of the elder Hamlet on his loss of the rites of the Church had its value, we may be sure, to the auditors in the Globe Theatre. It has its value to-day, not only to persons who have the historical sense, but to many who can see — whether we admit that Shakespeare's conception of the Ghost was strictly theological or not — that he realized what was meant by the cutting off of a

Christian soul from its rights. Again, the Polonius of the modern theatre is a cross between a knave and a fool. It is true that Hamlet calls him a fool, but Hamlet in his fits of passion is not to be trusted. His picture of his uncle, for instance, — " Hyperion to a satyr," — and his underrating the qualities of a courageous, cool, highly intellectual, but deliberately bad man, as Claudius was, ought to show the representators that Hamlet's estimate of Polonius should be taken only as the estimate of an overwrought, almost maddened, and supersensitive soul. Polonius was shrewd, capable of deep thought, cultured, after the older fashion of the Euphuists; and a closer study of the influences that made him possible would prevent the actors or the managers from misrepresenting his creator's idea.

In the Prologue of the first act of Henry V, when Shakespeare despairs of crowding the splendid pageant of Agincourt into the theatre, he exclaims against the limits of the stage:

> Can this cockpit hold
> The vasty fields of France ? or may we cram
> Within this wooden O the very casques

> That did affright the air at Agincourt?
> O, pardon! since a crooked figure may
> Attest in little place a million;
> And let us, ciphers to this great accompt,
> On your imaginary forces work.
> Suppose within the girdle of these walls
> Are now confined two mighty monarchies,
> Whose high upreared and abutting fronts
> The perilous narrow ocean parts asunder:
> Piece out our imperfections with your thoughts;
> Into a thousand parts divide one man,
> And make imaginary puissance:
> Think, when we talk of horses, that you see them
> Printing their proud hoofs i' the receiving earth.

As a rule, Shakespeare adapts his dramas to the bounds of his theatrical world without any evident dissatisfaction with them. In fact, if his means of satisfying the sight had been greater, our pleasure in reading his plays would have been less.

No better example can be found in "Hamlet" of the loss the student suffers from the absence of the business used by the actors in the days of Elizabeth and James than in the first scene of the third act. Hamlet has unveiled his doubtful mind, and suddenly he sees Ophelia. A flood of sudden tenderness sweeps over his heart:

> Soft you now!
> The fair Ophelia! Nymph, in thy orisons
> Be all my sins remember'd.

It almost seems as if the wide-spread delusion that Hamlet is really mad were founded mainly on this scene; for here, unless some adequate reason for his suspicion of Ophelia's truth could be given to the auditors, he seems to be not only mad, but possessed of a brutal and sullen devil. It is enough for the close student of the play to believe, after careful comparison of various parts of the text, that Hamlet had come to distrust all women, and that he was vowed to "wipe away all trivial fond records"; but it is not enough for the average auditor, and we may be sure that there was some business arranged to explain obviously the Prince's outburst of wrath, after a moment, too, of extreme tenderness. The stage direction is simply "Exeunt King and Polonius." But where do they go for their "lawful espials"? Behind the arras? Into a gallery at the back of a room in the castle? The author sees that their presence must be made known to Hamlet, in order that he may have an excuse for acting the part of madness with such brutality. He must have some plain proof that Ophelia is playing upon him for the benefit of her father, and the anditors, according to the usage of the stage, must know that he has this proof; therefore it is the custom, in many stage presentments of the play, to reveal accidentally, for a moment, the presence of the King and Polonius. The insults of Hamlet — excusable only in a madman or one feigning madness — are directed then, not at the fair and gentle Ophelia, but at the listeners.

"I did love you once," he says with a breaking voice, and he adds, remembering, "I loved you not."

"I was the more deceived," Ophelia answers gently.

Then Hamlet, fearing his own weakness, frightens Ophelia with his accusations against himself. Her gentle face appeals to him, and he puts her to the test:

"Where's your father?"

"At home, my lord."

With the sensitive instinct of love, his face has read in Ophelia's that she is deceiving him.

There is no relenting after that. He loves her still, but he knows that she has deceived him. To the winds he flings his wrath; the listeners must believe him mad, and she — "Frailty, thy name is woman."

Considered as a play, treated as intelligent actors who desired simply to bring out its meaning would treat it, "Hamlet" ceases to be a puzzle. It must be remembered, however, that, until the historical sense is cultivated in the theatres, light thrown on certain passages by the actor's instinct and insight will not pierce other passages equally worthy of illumination.

THE GREATEST OF SHAKE-
SPEARE'S CONTEMPORARIES

THE GREATEST OF SHAKE-SPEARE'S CONTEMPORARIES

IT is not strange that American and English writers of plays should seize their material as they do, but it is amazing that our modern dramatists should appropriate with so little discretion. While every tyro in the dramatic art rushes to Feuillet and Dumas for situations and motives, and forgotten comedies written when Mademoiselle Fargueil was in her prime are dismembered by the scissors of the modern dramatist, Lope de Vega and Calderon, who left innumerable treasures, and later Spanish dramatists of great merit are neglected. As the rage for play-writing is now at its height, the seeker after dramatic situations would do well to drop his search for French novelties and turn his attention toward that magnificent national outgrowth of the most magnificent nation of Europe, the Spanish drama. Beside it French dramatic art is stilted and colorless; "Faust" loses much, because it eternally questions and never answers; Greek dramatic art, individual and strong, does not dwarf it; for Calderon, the greatest dramatic poet of Spain, lacked only the humor of Shakespeare to have been the greatest dramatic poet of the world.

The political revolt of Henry VIII did for a time much intellectual harm to all of us who have inherited the English tongue, by narrowing our literary sympathies. Sectarian narrowness caused Calderon to be only a name, more or less connected with the Inquisition, and consequently disreputable, and made us content with a small portion of the glorious inheritance which Catholic Spain has left us. It would be absurd to claim that Calderon was a poet because he was a Catholic, but it is certain that Dante and he would never have been great poets had they not been Catholics. They were glorious flowers blooming at the end of a glorious Summer. Around them were the tinted leaves of decay which hid in false splendor the track of death; their roots were not nourished by the sun-dried soil around them; they struck deeper and were vivified by eternal springs. The influences about them would have made Dante a weaver of conceits, and Calderon an inventor of court spectacles. Mediæval Christianity strengthened their inspiration. As Emerson has it:

> The litanies of nations came,
> Like the volcano's tongue of flame,
> Up from the burning cave below —
> The canticles of love and woe;
> The hand that rounded Peter's dome,
> And groined the aisles of Christian Rome,
> Wrought in a sad sincerity:
> Himself from God he could not free.

God, the Trinity, our Lord, true God and true man, His blessed Mother, and the saints, are always with Calderon. The teaching of the Church was the pivot upon which all his world swung; her life filled his heart and soul. Humanity might ask questions and nature present problems, but Calderon always found their answer and solution in religion. It is this characteristic of the great Spanish poet which causes Frederick Schlegel to exclaim: " In this great and divine master the enigma of life is not only expressed but solved." But the Schlegels were smitten with that Calderon fever against which Goethe protested, and their indiscriminate praise has done his reputation as much harm as the coldness, prejudice, and ignorance of Sismondi and Hallam. Hallam, however, was only ignorant of Calderon's real merit, while Sismondi was evidently prejudiced. It may seem ridiculous, but it seems nevertheless true, that if the fact that Dante put popes into the *inferno* had not given the Italian master a piquant flavor, he would not have become so well known among us. Even Dean Trench, who has written a valuable and sympathetic essay on Calderon, approaches his "autos," or religious dramas, hesitatingly, and, broadminded as the Dean is, he constantly offers apologies to his prejudices by carefully explaining that he does not admire Calderon's "Romanism." After having made this plain he says: "And it is not too much to say of the greater number of these marvellous compositions that they are hymns of loftiest praise to redeeming love, summonses to all things which have breath to praise the Lord; and he, too, that writes, writes as one that has seen Satan fall like lightning from heaven, and rejoices in spirit with his Lord."

Calderon's "autos" were the perfection of the miracle-play, or "mystery," which was the national drama of Spain. With the skill of a trained dramatist (he was manager of the court theatre in the palace of the Buen Retiro) and the insight of a poet, he seized the parables of the Scriptures, the doctrines of the Church, the religious legends of the people, and even the heathen myths, and wrought them into these "autos" for the salvation of his countrymen. They might, indeed, rather be called moralities than mysteries. Every incident is arranged with almost mathematical precision, to the end that a moral may be taught. Lope de Vega, Calderon's predecessor, had done much to elevate the stage of the people; but Calderon, at once priest and dramatist, found both his vocations joined in the composition of his "autos." He could preach his sermons more effectively to the eye than to the ear. The Germans recognized the genius of Calderon with great cordiality, and Schiller regretted that he had not read him in earlier life. For a long time the only translations of any of these "autos" were in German. Until Denis Florence MacCarthy Englished the "Sorceries of Sin" none of the "autos" of Calderon had appeared in an English garb. Dean Trench had given an analysis of "The Great Theatre of the World," and several scenes, and Mr. Ticknor and others had given analyses of "autos"; "but," as Mr. MacCarthy says in his introduction to "The Sorceries," "the 'autos,' the most wonderful of all his productions, and the only ones, with but two exceptions, which the great poet himself thought worthy of revision, have been passed over, I may say, in almost utter silence."

The Germans, enthusiastic as they have shown themselves over the secular plays of Calderon, shrank from the task which Mr. MacCarthy completed with such thorough success. The characters in "Los Encantos de la Culpa," which is called a "sacramental allegorical auto," are the Man, Sin, Voluptuousness, Flattery, the Understanding, Penance, the

Smell, the Hearing, the Touch, the Taste, musicians, and chorus. The scene opens to the sound of the trumpet. A ship is discovered at sea. In it are the Man, the Understanding, and the Five Senses. The Understanding warns the Man that he is afloat on the world's wide sea and that a mighty tempest threatens him. The Senses then declare their characters, and act the part of the crew during the tempest, with wonderful dramatic spirit. The character of the play and its motive, in the hands of so religious a poet as Calderon, may be gathered from the title and the names of the *dramatis personæ*. But no analysis could do justice to the originality, the beauty, the simplicity, and the intense dramatic quality of this poetical drama. In this "auto" as in several others, Calderon uses the Greek mythology in a manner which shows his skill and his deep religious feeling. His fervor fuses the Christian religion and the myths, so that their pagan character is entirely lost. In the hands of a poet like Çamoëns the myths, mingled with Christian personages and symbols, produce a grotesque and profane effect.

Calderon seizes them boldly, as if by the divine right of a Christian. He illumines the faces of the gods with a new glory; he causes the pipe of Pan to join in the heavenly chorus, and makes Orpheus, whose music gives a new sense to the beasts, a figure of our Lord. "The True God Pan" is the title of one; another is founded on the story of Cupid and Psyche, and another on Ulysses and Circe. Most of his "autos" rest, however, on a Scriptural basis, such as "The Vineyard of the Lord," "The Wheat and the Tares," and "The Hid Treasures"; others on Old Testament facts — "The Brazen Serpent," "Gideon's Fleece," "The Sheaves of Ruth," and "Balthasar's Feast"; others, while strictly moral, are somewhat less Scriptural, — for instance, "Love the Greatest Enchantment" and "The Sorceries of Sin" are Christian dramatic allegories, both founded on the myth of Ulysses and Circe.

The richness of imagery, the wealth of fancy, and the firmness of grasp which the poet shows in working out these marvellous acts make each a precious heritage to poetry as well as to dramatic art. They are unique, and they merit a thorough study. A Catholic alone can sympathize with their spirit and revel in the deep religious life which fills them. A speech of Penance to Sin in " Los Encantos de la Culpa " will give an idea of the beauty of the drama. This passage loses nothing of its beauty in Mr. MacCarthy's interpretation :

> I,
> Erst who wore the rainbow's dress,
> Who if in a car triumphal
> Thou to-day behold'st me seated
> 'Neath a canopy, wherein
> Purple, pearl, and gold are blended,
> 'T is because I come to triumph
> Over thee; for whensoever
> Calleth me Man's Understanding,
> Never is the call neglected.
> All the virtues which he squandered
> In his ignorance demented
> I have here regathered, since
> Certain 't is that when presented
> By the hand of Grace they 've been,
> He who turneth back repentant
> Ever findeth them again,
> Safely guarded and preservèd.
> And that Man may know that they
> Can alone thy sorceries render
> Powerless, thou wilt now behold

All the viands here collected
Vanish into air, and leave
Naught behind to tell their presence;
Showing thus how human glory
Is as false as evanescent,
Since the only food that lasteth
Is the food for souls intended —
Is the eternal Bread of Life
Which now fills this table's centre.
It is Penance that presents it,
Since without her (naught more certain)
Man deserveth not to witness
So much glory manifested.
Yet, ye Senses, 't is not bread,
But a substance most transcendent:
It is Flesh and Blood; because
When the substance is dissevered
From the species, the White Host (*Hostia blanca*) then
But the accidents preserveth.

Sin. How canst thou expect to gain
Credence from thy outraged Senses,
When they come to understand
How you wrong them and offend them?
Smell, come here, and with thy sense
Taste this bread, this substance; tell me,
Is it bread or flesh?

(*The Senses approach.*)

The Smell. Its smell
Is the smell of bread.
Sin. Taste, enter. Try it thou.
The Taste. Its taste is plainly
That of bread.

Sin. Touch, come. Why tremble?
Say what's this thou touchest?
 The Touch. Bread.
 Sin. Sight, declare what thou discernest
In this object.
 The Sight. Bread alone.
 Sin. Hearing, thou, too, break in pieces
This material, which, as flesh,
Faith proclaims and Penance preacheth;
Let the fraction, by its noise,
Of their error undeceive them.
Say, is it so?
 The Hearing. Ungrateful Sin,
Though the noise in truth resembles
That of bread when broken, yet
Faith and Penance teach us better
It is flesh, and what they call it
I believe: that Faith asserteth
Aught is proof enough thereof.
 The Understanding. This one reason brings contentment
Unto me.
 Penance. O Man! why linger,
Now that hearing hath firm fettered
To the Faith thy Understanding?
Quick! regain the saving vessel
Of the Sovereign Church, and leave
Sin's so briefly sweet excesses.
Thou, Ulysses, Circe's slave,
Fly this false and fleeting revel,
Since how great her power may be,
Greater is the power of Heaven,
And the true Jove's mightier magic
Will thy virtuous purpose strengthen.

The Man. Yes, thou 'rt right, O Understanding!
Lead in safety hence my Senses.
  All. Let us to our ship ; for here
All is shadowy and unsettled.
  Sin. What imports it, woe is me ! —
What imports it that my sceptre
Thus you seem to 'scape from, since
My enchantments will attend you ?
I shall rouse the waves to madness.
  Penance. I shall follow and appease them.

(*Trumpets peal. The ship is discovered, and all go on board.*)

The "auto" ends with the triumph of Penance over the enchantments of Circe, and, this new Ulysses having escaped, the *dramatis personæ* sing:

> Let this mightiest miracle
> Over all the world be fêted,
> Specially within Madrid,
> City where Spain's proud heart swelleth,
> Which, in honoring God's body,
> Takes the foremost place for ever.

In another "auto," "The Great Theatre of the World," Calderon takes for his theme,

> En el teatro del mundo
> Todos son representados,

which Shakespeare had already rendered:

> All the world 's a stage,
> And all the men and women merely players.

In the beginning the author summons his people, the Rich Man, the Beggar, the King, the Husbandman, the Beauty, the Hermit, or Discretion, and the Infant. They receive their parts from him, with the words,

> Act your best, for God is God,

and a sublime drama of life goes on. Dean Trench[1] has given an interesting analysis of this "auto," to which we refer the reader who is too indolent to rub up his Spanish.

Calderon was born in 1600, either in the beginning of January or February, although his friend Vera Tassis makes the year of his birth 1601. "Los Hijos de Madrid" (Calderon first saw the light in Madrid) gives February 14, 1600, as the day of his baptism. Another work quoted by Dean Trench, "Obelisco Funebre," states, on the authority of the poet himself, that he was born January 17, 1600. His parents, according to the

[1] Calderon, by R. C. Trench.

chronicles of the time, were Christian and prudent people, who, being of illustrious lineage, gave their children an education in conformity with it. His father held a State office under Philip II and Philip III. Don Pedro, the poet, was the youngest of four children. His brother Diego succeeded to the family estate, his sister entered the Order of St. Clare, and José fell in battle in 1645. He learned the rudiments in the Jesuit College of Madrid. Afterwards he studied — some biographers say for five years — philosophy and theology at the famous University of Salamanca. No one can read any play of Calderon's without being impressed with the deeply religious bent of his mind, and with the evidence of theological study which each of them displays. To the *Summa* of St. Thomas he owed all that certainty and firmness in grasping the great questions of life which was the despair of Schiller and the admiration of Goethe. Well might Augustus Schlegel, who, unlike his brother Frederick, had not accepted the Church, exclaim: "Blessed man! he had escaped from the wild labyrinths of doubt into the stronghold of belief; thence, with undisturbed tranquillity of soul, he beheld and portrayed the storms of the world. To him human life was no longer a dark riddle."

When the crown fell from Shakespeare's dying head in England, Calderon had scarcely begun to sing in Spain. He lived to pass the threescore and ten allotted to man by eleven years. While the drama degenerated into spectacular and intellectually valueless shows in Spain, it likewise degenerated in England into the bastard, the soulless, the heartless comedy of the Restoration. He lived to see the Spanish theatre, which he had built, following Lope de Vega, to a most noble height, become a mere vehicle for *tours de force* of scenic effects. And he does not seem to have been conscious of this degradation. He even helped it along.

Nothing could have been more repellent to his nature than the polished yet open obscenity of the English comedies in vogue in his latter years. He would have been quick to perceive the evil tendency of the wit of Congreve and Wycherley, and to raise his voice against it; but he failed to see that the splendid spectacles which he offered to the eyes of the court on the great pond of the Buen Retiro were as ruinous to the intellectual enjoyment of the drama as licentiousness and frivolity. To the glory of this most noble-minded of poets it must be said that no *double entente*, no vile allusion or coarse pun such as Shakespeare felt himself too often bound to introduce, often making of great passages "sweet bells jangled," ever appears in the works of Calderon. Yet Calderon was the boldest of dramatists — bolder, because purer and without any self-conscious delight in shocking his audience, than the boldest of the French Romanticists.

"The Devotion of the Cross," a powerful drama, contains scenes which in a less firm and pure hand would have left that sense of despair which we feel at the end of a great Greek play when the Fates have done their work. The impression derived from Sismondi that this sublime play turns on the crime of incest is false; and it is surprising that even the most careless reader could have failed to see that Eusebio and Julia, guilty though they were, were saved from this unutterable crime. And in the scene, as translated by Mr. MacCarthy, in which they are saved, the masterly character of Calderon's art shows itself. It requires the highest purity of purpose and the aid of great genius to produce the effect of horror on the spectator's mind — the horror which the witness of a great crime feels — without vulgarizing the intensity of the horror or degrading the audience by forcing them to sympathize momentarily with the crime.

Another Spanish writer possessed this high purpose and this art, though in her case talent supplied the place of genius. Readers of "La Gaviota" of Fernan Caballero will remember instances of it. It is easy to make an audience thrill with sympathy for temptation, or crime which is the result of passion, and the effects of too many of the romantic dramatists have been produced in this cheap way; but it is not easy to cause the sin to be abhorred while the audience is still in sympathy with those who are on the verge of committing it. Calderon, of all dramatists, was master of the means of producing this effect. Pure as his intent always was, and thoroughly Catholic as he everywhere shows himself to be, yet he did not hesitate to touch the most secret springs of passion. A skilful master of stage tricks, he was never misled into vulgar and easy effects. All his situations were planned most artfully, nothing was left to chance; and consequently the interest lies in the action of the drama, not in its characters. Calderon was a court poet and dramatist, and the result of habitual contact with the members of the most ceremonious and stately court in Europe is often apparent in his plays.

It is, therefore, amusing to read Voltaire's complaints of the natural and uncultivated nature of the Spanish drama; and Voltaire's opinion of the Spanish drama is as valuable as his allusion to Hamlet as "a drunken Dane." Nothing could be more artificial than the structure of Calderon's dramas. They are geometrical in their precision; some of them seem to be founded on a scholastic formula; but nevertheless Calderon probes the depth of the human heart and holds in his disciplined hand the key to all the passions. French critics, always having the reverence for their Louis Quatorze imitations of the Greek drama before their eyes, could not appreciate Calderon. They found him too spontaneous, almost savage, because his rules of dramatic art differed from theirs.

Dean Trench quotes a critical opinion from a book published in Paris in 1669, "Journal de Voyage d'Espagne," in which the complacent French traveller says: "Yesterday came the Marquis of Eliche, eldest son of Don Luis De Haro, and Monsieur de Barrière, and took me to the theatre. The play, which had been before brought forward but was newly revived, was naught, although it had Don Pedro Calderon for author. At a later hour I made a visit to this Calderon, who is held the greatest poet and most illustrious genius in Spain at the present day. He is knight of the Order of Santiago and chaplain to the Chapel of the Kings at Toledo; but I gathered from his conversation that his head-piece was furnished poorly enough. We disputed a good while on the rules of the drama, which in this land are not recognized, and about which the Spaniards make themselves merry." But the critic of to-day, recalling how Calderon, in spite of his strict rules and courtly elegance, touched the hearts of the common people, will differ from the French interviewer and thank Heaven that this Spanish poet triumphed over more hampering regulations than ever bound Racine or Corneille.

The boldness with which he handled his *motifs* and characters excited the ill nature and reckless censure of Sismondi, who finds in "The Devotion of the Cross" much that would be, if it were there, abominable. "On devine sans peine que Julia est la sœur d'Eusèbe; et cette invention dramatique augmentant d'intensité irait coudoyer l'horreur et l'insoutenable, si Calderon n'était doué de ce vrai génie dont l'essence est pure. Nous allons le voir, dans une occasion si difficile retrouver la moralité qui lui est propre, la sublime pudeur qui ne l'abandonne jamais. Ses ailes blanches et vierges trempent dans l'orage sans le flétrir, et effleurent la foudre sans se brûler." The truth of this last beautiful sentence is often forced upon the reader. The "white and spotless wings" of this genius flutter amid darkness and storm unsullied and unruffled. In a turmoil of passion and jealousy, such as "Physician of his Own Honor," of which there is a French version, he remains calm and pure while his hearers shudder with horror. His plays of which jealousy is the theme seem to have been torn from a living and burning heart. They are almost unendurably horrible, yet they are wonders of dramatic art; and in the warring of the elements Calderon never changes his plan or loses his grasp. Either the taste of the Spanish court was much less coarse than that of the English, or Calderon's elevating studies of the *Summa* must have made him disdain low things; for although Cervantes and, it is said, the pleasant *farceur*, Tirso de Molina, often made allusions which in any age would have been considered indecent, Calderon's works are free from these blots.

Señor Hartzenbusch tells us that Calderon was nineteen when he left Salamanca, and surmises that "The Devotion of the Cross" was written before he left the University. In it he expresses the difficulty of pleasing an audience variously composed, in the speech beginning, "Copla hay tambien para ti," etc.

> Take this rhyme along with thee:
> Since, howe'er the poet tries,
> Doubtful is his drama's fate,
> For what may the crowd elate
> The judicious may despise.
> If you 're seeking for fame's prizes,
> Try some method less remote,
> For 't is hard to cut a coat
> That will suit all sorts of sizes.

Calderon did not despise the applause of the populace because he wrote for the approbation of the knights. He pleased both. He interested the people, in spite of themselves, in the heroism that the Moors had displayed; this was not the least of his triumphs. "The Chariot of Heaven," his first play, written when he was fourteen, has not come down to us. At the age of twenty-five we find him serving in the Low Countries as a soldier, as Cervantes and Garcilasso the lyric poet and other Spanish writers had served. In 1625 he was still in the army, if his "Siege of Breda," a military drama, may stand as evidence of his presence at the taking of that town. Philip IV, a *littérateur* and a lover of the drama, summoned him to court. In 1630 Lope de Vega acknowledged that his mantle had fallen on the poet-soldier, and on Lope's death, five years later, there was no one left to dispute the bays with Calderon. Calderon was a favorite at court. His lines were cast in pleasant places. The light of the courtly glare in which he lived did not wither his genius; it was good for him; he throve in the splendor, and flourished. Unlike so many of his brethren, he had no struggles with fate. The spectacular pieces which his position as director of the court theatre in the palace of the Buen Retiro forced him to prepare are the weakest and the most unsatisfactory of his productions.

Ben Jonson's masques, which were fashionable at the English court at this time, were somewhat similar, but in some respects more meritorious. Calderon, who doubtless felt the arrangement of these magnificent shows a heavy task, avenged himself by torturing the stage machinist. "Circe," which was represented on the great pond of the Buen Retiro on St. John's Night, 1635, is accompanied with most elaborate directions which would drive the very modern stage manager to despair. Here is a sample:

"In the midst of this island will be situated a very lofty mountain of rugged ascent, with precipices and caverns, surrounded by a thick and darksome wood of tall trees, some of which will be seen to exhibit the appearance of the human form covered with a rough bark, from the heads and arms of which will issue green boughs and branches, having suspended from them various trophies of war and of the chase, the theatre, during the opening of the scene, being scantily lit with concealed lights; and, to make a beginning of the festival, a murmuring and a rippling noise of water having been heard, a great and magnificent car will be seen to advance along the pond, plated over with silver, and drawn by two monstrous fishes, from whose mouths will continually issue great jets of water, the light of the theatre increasing according as they advance; and on the summit of it will be seated in great pomp and majesty the goddess Aqua, from whose head and curious vesture will issue an infinite abundance of little conduits of water; and at the same time will be seen another great supply flowing from an urn which the goddess will hold reversed, and which, filled with a variety of fishes, that, leaping and playing in the torrent as it descends and gliding over all the car, will fall into the pond."

This is only a glimmer of the wonders to follow. Calderon spared no expense on these spectacles, and the king seems to have been lavish in his expenditures for adding decorations and mechanism of the newest pattern to the paraphernalia of the court theatre. Being a member of the military order of Santiago, Calderon entered the field in 1637 to help to suppress a revolt in one of the provinces. How long he remained in the army is not certain; it is plain, however, that Philip IV preferred that he should remain at court. He gave up the pursuit of arms, although he still clung to that of literature, and received holy orders. His genius was of so sacred a kind that he needed not to throw aside his pen to take up the cross. His works were psalms, and he only needed the added grace of the Christian priesthood to make him a perfect symbol of Catholic art. His life had been calm and happy — or as calm and happy as the life of such a man, whose eyes were fixed on God and who knew no real contentment not seeing God, could be. On Whitsunday, May 25, 1681, he died, no longer a court favorite, — for Philip had died in 1665, — but revered and loved. He was buried in the Church of San Salvadore at Madrid. The glimpses which we get of him from his contemporaries are few, but they make us feel that his life was noble and that his works reflected it. His relations with Lope de Vega and Cervantes (he dramatized " Don Quixote") were friendly and cordial. Not much is known of his ways among men, but what is known shows him to be a high type of a high and noble people.

With Calderon died the glory of Spain. Lope de Vega had modelled the statue out of rude stone, which Calderon had completed. Out of the national life of Spain had come the strong impulse which gave a new drama to the world, to take its place proudly beside the drama of Greece and the drama of England; which gave a New World to the Old, and drew from this New World those glittering streams that gilded but could not revive it. Materialism had hidden the cross and dimmed the old Spanish ideal. The gorgeous trappings of the body had almost smothered the soul. Calderon making spectacles for the court, while the enemies of Spain were dismembering her, and her soldiers in new lands sowing the seeds of hatred in the name of God, whom their lust outraged, was a symbol of his country, forgetting the ideal of other days and substituting for it empty splendor and worthless gold.

IMITATORS OF SHAKESPEARE

IMITATORS OF SHAKESPEARE

STUDENTS of literature are of one mind, even in the face of the vogue of Rostand's "Cyrano de Bergerac," Phillips's "Ulysses," and Shaw's "Candida," as to the evident decay of the literary element in most of the plays successfully performed at the theatres. The French still listen with respect to the masterpieces of Racine, Corneille, and Molière, but we must remember that the *Comédie Française* is a subsidized theatre. Molière was, like Shakespeare, both a man of letters and an actor. He knew the turn of the literary phrase, but he knew also how to give his phrase the dramatic touch without which the most splendid poetry falls echoless from the stage. Shakespeare had the dramatic power and the theatrical skill, and yet so different were the requirements of the Elizabethan stage from ours that no modern manager except Mr. Ben Greet dares to put a play of Shakespeare's forward without various necessary changes, and even he must "cut" many lines. Even so careful a manager as the late Mr. Augustin Daly took out the fine speech of the first lord in "As You Like It"[1] because it impedes the action of the play. Eloquence as eloquence, poetry as poetry, does not count on the modern stage. Words are no longer held to be the principal symbols which the dramatist must use for the presentation of his ideas. It is the psychological value of muscular expression — of action and the suggestion of emotion — that he must weigh.

He learns the value of the pause, of the glance of the eye, of the trembling of the hand, of the laugh, of the sob; he gauges the effect of silence itself; but for long speeches, for soliloquies that are merely eloquent or poetical, he has no use. They will not do. You may argue that this condition of affairs means degeneracy, and you will be met with Professor Brander Matthews's reply, — that the drama, as well as the other arts of

[1] Act II, Sc. 1.

sculpture and painting and music, ought not to be judged from a literary point of view. The dramatic quality may cause a play to live for the hour, and only for the hour; the literary quality gives it permanence; it is this quality which makes it eventually a classic. Professor Brander Matthews says:

"Nobody disputes that dramatic literature must be literature, although there are not a few who do not insist that it must be dramatic. The great dramatists have accepted this double obligation, and they have always recognized that the stage of the theatre, and not the desk of the library, is the true proving room. This double obligation it is that makes the drama so difficult an art, perhaps, indeed, the most difficult of all arts."

The great dramatists to whom Professor Brander Matthews alludes are easily enumerated, and they are very great indeed, — Calderon, Lope de Vega, Shakespeare, Racine, Corneille, Schiller, Molière, and Goldsmith; for Goldsmith in "She Stoops to Conquer" has left us at least one play that answers both the literary and the dramatic tests. Scores of other dramatists who held the theatre in their day and delighted their fellows are forgotten. Before the footlights their characters lived; in the book-shelves they are very like the dried sea-weed, which takes on color and life only in its congenial element. Taken from the stage, they have no life, no interest; they are as dry as the dust in which they repose.

On the other hand, there are scores of brilliant dramas which live only in the letter; which, although not written for the closet, can be endured only in the study. They contain the highest poetry, the most thrilling eloquence; they are talked about rather than read. And when one hears a line from them, one is rather certain to be able to trace it to a dictionary of quotations. And these noble works of poetic art are forgotten, except as to their names, because their authors were poets, but not dramatists. The conditions of the stage have changed, and Sophocles and Shakespeare and Racine do not fit well in the atmosphere of our modern theatre. The method of Shakespeare, who is careful to indicate locality and time and physical surroundings in his text, is the method of the modern novelist rather than of the modern dramatist; hence the necessity of "adapting" him to the exigencies of the modern theatre; just as a novel, no matter how much essential dramatic quality there may be in it, must be arranged for the stage. The essential dramatic quality is important, but an acting play must succeed or fall through the *presentment* of the dramatic quality. "It is the vast power a good actor has in this way," Sir Henry Irving said, in his address before the Philosophical Institute of Edinburgh, "which has led the French to speak of creating a part when they mean its first being played; and the French authors are so conscious of the extent and value of this coöperation of actors with them, that they have never objected to the phrase, but, on the contrary, are uniformly lavish in their homage to the artists who have created on the boards the parts which they themselves have created on paper."

The characters, then, are conceived by the author; they are grouped by him in accordance with the dramatic laws of logic and movement; but unless he knows these laws, unless he can project himself into the minds of his auditors, unless he is sure that contrast and action are his main tools, he cannot succeed in making a drama for the stage. He must be capable of perceiving the dramatic worth of our knowledge that Lady Teazle is behind the screen in that marvellously constructed scene in Sheridan's "School for Scandal"; he can leave nothing to chance, as Shakespeare leaves nothing to chance in the trial scene in "The Merchant of Venice"; but he must leave much to interpretation.

On the other hand, the names of Shelley, Sir Henry Taylor, Browning, Swinburne, and the two De Veres, must be uttered by men of letters with respect; and yet they failed as dramatists. They produced "closet" dramas,—dramas invented for a stage that does not exist, modelled on Elizabethan forms, without the inner power of appealing to the dramatic sense. As dramas, "The Cenci" of Shelley, "A Blot in the 'Scutcheon," "Strafford," and "Luria," of Browning, "Mary Stuart" and "Chastelard" of Swinburne, "Philip van Artevelde" and "Edwin the Fair" of Sir Henry Taylor, the "Mary Tudor" of Sir Aubrey de Vere, the "Alexander the

Great" and "St. Thomas of Canterbury" of Aubrey Thomas de Vere, the "Queen Mary" and "Becket" of Tennyson, are "closet" dramas. To quote Mr. Crawford's happy phrase, they are plays for a "pocket theatre." Of all these great men Tennyson made the most violent effort to be theatrical, and a very great failure. "Harold" and "Queen Mary" and "Becket" are neither great poems nor great dramas. Shelley's "Cenci," in spite of the repellent subject, is a classic, — beautiful, glowing, terrible. Browning's "Strafford" and "Luria" and "A Blot in the 'Scutcheon" are literature, but they have not the acting quality; they are not objective. "His stage," Mr. Henry Brown says, in "Browning as a Dramatic Poet," "is filled with moral agents in a state of moral tension, not with men and women who are flesh and blood as well as spirit." Swinburne's tragedies are hard reading, though full of eloquence and lyrical quality, and the "Philip van Artevelde" of Sir Henry Taylor and "Mary Tudor" of Sir Aubrey de Vere, have some magnificent poetical passages, but they lack every requirement for the acting play. "Richelieu" and "The Lady of Lyons," though they hold the stage, are not literature, nor is "Caste," or "Held by the Enemy," or "The Way of the World,"[1] or "The Henrietta," or "Alabama," or "Shore Acres," or any of the popular favorites; but they are plays which appeal to us as the orator appeals to us, — for an hour or two, and then the fire dies away.

Permit me to compare two plays written by two very great poets, — Tennyson's "Becket" and Aubrey Thomas de Vere's "St. Thomas of Canterbury," to show that the highest poetical quality will not save a noble play from being of the "closet," that is, study type, and that the poet who tries to make a great subject dramatic by lowering it to what he deems to be the popular theatrical demand, fails. Tennyson sacrificed the truth of history and the truth of character in attempting to theatricalize the character of Thomas of Canterbury, with the consequence that, if "Becket" and the dramas in which he has followed a similar process were lost, his reputation would be the better for it.

[1] Clyde Fitch.

In picturesqueness and grace the
"Becket" of the late laureate is vastly
superior to the one which, after "Alexander the Great," has made Aubrey Thomas
de Vere's name glorious in the literary
annals of the nineteenth century. But a
great tragedy on a subject which is what
the Germans call "epoch-making" demands higher qualities than picturesqueness and that nameless grace and delicacy
so essentially Tennysonian. It needs
even higher qualities than the contrast
of marked characters, pointed epigrams,
or the fine play of poetic fancy. Lord
Tennyson's "Becket" has all the lower
qualities, Aubrey Thomas de Vere's "St.
Thomas of Canterbury" all the higher.
An oak is not more of an oak because
the sward around is starred by violets and
all the blooms of Spring; and De Vere's
"St. Thomas" would not be a greater
tragedy if it had the exquisite touches
which the most delicate master of poetic
technique the world has ever seen gave to
"Becket."

Tennyson's tragedy is meant to be
an acting play; De Vere's is, frankly,
a drama for the study. The lack of

nobility in Tennyson's is due to the necessity he felt of making it fit the arbitrary refinements of the stage.

The episode of Fair Rosamond, which is an offence against historical truth, good art, and taste, would never have been introduced had the late laureate not been required to give a leading dramatic lady something to do. Still, writers impregnated with certain prejudices are always crying, *Cherchez la femme*. If a man is holy, and there is no disputing the fact, they construct a romance with a woman in it to account for his renunciations. Tennyson has ruined a magnificent *persona* by making him, on the eve of his death for Christianity and liberty, drivel of what he might have gained had he married. In the monastery at Canterbury, just before the tolling of the bell that calls him to his doom, he sighs:

> There was a little fair-haired Norman maid
> Lived in my mother's house: if Rosamond is
> The world's rose, as her name imports her, she
> Was the world's lily.
> *John of Salisbury.* Ay, and what of her?
> *Becket.* She died of leprosy.
> *John of Salisbury.*   I know not why
> You call these old things back, my lord.

Becket. The drowning man, they say, remembers all
The chances of his life, just ere he dies.

Surely the poet who gave us a type of purity in Sir Galahad, and of chaste elevation in King Arthur, might have better understood the character of the successor of St. Anselm. It is impossible to approach the climax, or rather anti-climax, of Tennyson's play without impatience and irritation. If

> To be wroth with one we love
> Doth work like madness in the brain,

the discovery that a true poet has misunderstood a grand character and frittered away a sublime opportunity is an incentive, too, to a helpless, hopeless sort of anger.

In De Vere's "St. Thomas" there is no anti-climax, no disappointment. We miss sometimes the flowers that might grow around the foot of the oak, but the oak towers majestic. "St. Thomas" possesses what many of us thought lacking in the less ambitious poems of an author who has given out much light without heat, sustained intensity of passion. Added to this, De Vere thoroughly understood the historical meaning of St. Thomas's time, and the relations of the great Chancellor and Primate to that time. Of these the laureate seemed to be in the densest ignorance, or he hid his knowledge for theatrical effect. If in "Queen Mary" he drew his facts from Froude, and in "Harold," it seems, from Bulwer Lytton, he appears in "Becket" to have depended on his own inner consciousness for his history. He has in the most important particulars ignored the authentic chronicles of his time.

It was, indeed, an "epoch-making" time, and one worthy of a grand commemoration in an immortal poem. England owed her liberty to the Church; and more than all, to St. Anselm and St. Thomas, because they first withstood the advancing waves of royal despotism. And the freedom of the Church was the freedom of the people. St. Anselm put into the "Mariale" the echoes of the wails of the Saxon people, beaten down by alien conquerors. The Saxons saw their priests made powerless, their Church enslaved, and themselves in hopeless serfdom, when suddenly that Christianity which knows no nationality, which fuses all nations into one, asserted her might in the persons of two primates, — one of the conquering race, the other of the foreigner's court. The position of St. Thomas à Becket has been misinterpreted so utterly that he is often set down as an ambitious revolutionist who tried, in the interests of ecclesiastical tyranny, to dominate both King and people. In truth, the Archbishop of Canterbury struggled for old English laws against new ones devised by the Normans to rivet more closely the fetters of serfdom on the Saxon people.

It has been made a reproach against St. Thomas that he resisted the "Royal Customs," that he figured as a haughty prince of the Church scorning the pretensions of the Plantagenet, and that he died a martyr to his obstinate desire to crush even royal freedom, that he and his monks might triumph. This view is founded on a misconception of the nature of the Royal Customs. They were not old Customs, but innovations invented by the conquerors for their autocratic purposes. De Vere puts into Becket's mouth a graphic description of these famous Customs. The Earl of Cornwall says:

> You serve the king
> Who stirred these wars? who spurned the Royal Customs?
>
> *Becket.* The Customs — ay, the Customs? We have reached
> At last — 't was time — the inmost of this plot,
> Till now so deftly veiled and ambushed. "Customs"!
> O specious word, how plausibly abused!
> In Catholic ears that word is venerable;
> To Catholic souls custom is law itself,
> Law that its own foot hears not, dumbly treading
> A holy path smoothed by traditions old.
> I war not, sirs, on way traditionary;
> The Church of Christ herself is a tradition;
> Ay, 't is God's tradition, not of men!
> Sir, these your Customs are God's laws reversed,
> Traditions making void the Word of God,
> Old innovations from the first withstood,
> The rights of holy Church, the poor man's portion,
> Sold, and for naught, to aliens. Customs! Customs!
> Custom was that which to the lord of the soil
> Yielded the virgin one day wedded! Customs!
> A century they have lived; but he ne'er lived,
> The man that knew their number or their scope,
> Where found, by whom begotten, or how named:
> Like malefactors long they hid in holes;
> They walked in mystery like the noontide pest;
> In the air they danced; they hung on breath of princes,
> Largest when princes' lives were most unclean,

And visible most when rankest was the mist.
Sirs, I defy your Customs: they are naught.
I turn from them to our old English laws,
The Confessor's and those who went before him,
The charters old, and sacred oaths of kings:
I clasp the tables twain of Sinai:
On them I lay my palms, my heart, my forehead,
And on the altars dyed by martyrs' blood,
Making to God appeal.

These usages of tyranny were the Customs that St. Thomas resisted to death. Indeed throughout the whole of his work De Vere departs from the chronicled truth in nothing, except in the episode of Idonea de Lisle, the ward of Becket's sister. Idonea, a rich heiress, pursued by the ruffianly knight De Broc, who "roamed a-preying on the race of men," took refuge with Becket's sister and was protected by the power of the Primate. De Broc gained the King's ear, and, "on some pretence of law," drove Idonea from the house of Becket's sister. De Broc and his friends sued for her as a royal ward; judgment went against her, and we are told that she escaped only by becoming a postulant.

Judgment against her went. The day had come,
And round the minster knights and nobles watched:

> The chimes rang out at noon : then from the gate
> Becket walked forth, the maiden by his side :
> Ay, but her garb conventional showed the nun !
> They frowned, but dared no more.

The feminine interest, to give which to his tragedy Tennyson invented a new version of the legend of Fair Rosamond, is supplied by De Vere in this very fitting episode of Idonea. It is artistic and congruous, but unless put into action it would not do for the stage. Idonea is exiled from England when the King's wrath bursts on all the relatives, friends, and dependants of À Becket; she finds refuge with the Empress Matilda, mother of the King. Then occurs a scene between the Empress and the novice, which, for spiritual as well as intellectual elevation, has seldom been equalled.

One would think that it would have been easy to give the necessary feminine element to "Becket" by the use of an underplot; but Tennyson has preferred to bring the King's mistress, a "light o' love," Fair Rosamond, into intimate association with the Archbishop of Canterbury, whose purity, even before he took orders, amid all the temptations of the court, presided over by a loose-minded Provençal Queen, was proverbial. Fair Rosamond is rehabilitated for the purpose of the laureate. She is made to be, in her own eyes, the lawful wife of King Henry; and the Chancellor — not yet made Primate — promises the King to protect her against the vengeance of Queen Eleanor.

Becket, having become Primate and gained the hatred of the King, does so; and, in a dagger-scene quite worthy of a sensational play, saves her from Eleanor's fury. After that he induces her to leave her son and begin a novitiate in Godstow convent, from which she emerges, with the consent of the abbess, disguised as a monk. She is thus present at the murder of the Archbishop, and her presence excites that tender retrospection so in keeping with theatrical traditions, but so shockingly contrary to the martyr's character and the truth of history. It is here that Becket says, according to Tennyson:

> Dan John, how much we lose, we celibates,
> Lacking the love of woman and of child!

John of Salisbury seeks to give the Archbishop consolation for his supposed loss, in a most ungallant and pessimistic tone smacking somewhat of "sour grapes," in which he reminds St. Thomas that he might have married the wrong woman.

> More gain than loss ; for of your wives you shall
> Find one slut, whose fairest linen seems
> Foul as her dust-cloth, if she used it ; one
> So charged with tongue, that every thread of thought
> Is broken ere it joins ; a shrew to boot,
> Whose evil song far on into the night
> Thrills to the topmost tile — no hope but death ;
> One slow, fat, white, a burthen of the hearth ;
> And one that, being thwarted, ever swoons
> And weeps herself into a place of power.

This is hardly the way in which a sturdy and ascetic priest and counsellor would talk to an archbishop who, almost at the moment of martyrdom, would begin to look back at his "lost chances" of matrimony. How different, but how true, is the note struck by De Vere! Becket has been just made Primate, and he bursts into a splendid speech to Herbert of Bosham :

> Herbert ! my Herbert !
> High visions, mine in youth, upbraid me now ;
> I dreamed of sanctities redeemed from shame ;
> Abuses crushed ; all sacred offices
> Reserved for spotless hands. Again I see them ;

I see God's realm so bright, each English home
Showing that glory basks amid its peace :
I see the clear flame on the poor man's hearth
From God's own altar lit ; the angelic childhood ;
The chaste, strong youth ; the reverence of white hairs ;
'T is this Religion means.   O Herbert ! Herbert !
We must secure her this.   Her rights, the lowest,
Shall in my hand be safe.   I will not suffer
The pettiest stone in castle, grange, or mill,
The humblest clod of English earth, one time
A fief of my great mother, Canterbury,
To rest a caitiff's booty.   Herbert, Herbert,
Had I foreseen, with what a vigilant care
Had I built up my soul !

Becket's pupil, young Prince Henry, is heard singing without, and the Archbishop says, in contrast to the whines put into his mouth by Tennyson:

Hark to that truant's song !   We celibates
Are strangely captured by this love of children.
Nature's revenge — say, rather, compensation.

Exiled in the Abbey of Pontigny, after the King has poured his wrath on him and his kindred for defending the liberties of the Church and the people, he does not break out into wild regret or sentimental sighs.   There is a manly tenderness in his tone to the abbot:

My mother, when I went to Paris first,
A slender scholar bound on quest of learning,
Girding my gown collegiate, wept full sore,
Then laid on me this hest : Both early and late
To love Christ's Mother and the poor of Christ.
That so her prayer in heaven and theirs on earth,
Beside me moving as I walked its streets,
Might shield me from its sins.
    Abbot.   Men say your mother
Loved the poor well, and still on festivals,
Lay her growing babe in counter-scale,
Heaped up an equal weight of clothes and food,
Which unto them she gave.

De Vere's conception of the motives of the martyred Primate is worthy of the subject. Tennyson grasps only faintly the Christianity of À Becket. In the dialogue between the Abbot of Pontigny and the exiled Archbishop, just quoted, there is an example of Christian belief which, like sustaining gold threads in a tissue of silk, runs through the wonderful tragedy of De Vere's. The Chancellor is made Primate; he becomes less gay, less worldly, more given to the building up of his soul and mind, and more spiritual. He, almost alone, stands up for the Church and the people. Timeserving court bishops cower; the very court of Rome — but not the Church — seems to desert him. The Pope himself sends him the habit of the monks of Pontigny, with the cowl filled with snow — " the Pope knows well some heads are hot." The Archbishop endures it all with the meekness of a saint, yet with the dignity of a man. Through all trials, up to the time of martyrdom, he seems marked for special grace. He is not singularly learned, for the practical duties of the kingdom have left him little time for study. And yet he is well equipped with fortitude, and his hope never falters. Why? We are answered: Because his mother has loved God and the poor, and because he so loves Christ's poor, following her behest. This point is accentuated most sharply and artistically by the author.

Tennyson draws very sharply the envious and fawning prelates around the King, and his characterization is as keen and delicate as we have had every reason to expect it to be. But the virtuous priests in " Becket " are certainly a strange group. We know that the Church in England, half enslaved by the State and burdened with growing wealth, had need of reforms in discipline. De Vere, with a regard for truth which has probably caused guileless non-Catholics to expect to see him crushed by the Thunder of Rome, accentuates these facts. Matilda says:

> I would your primate
> Had let the Royal Custom be, and warred
> Against the ill customs of the Church. 'T is shame
> To ordain a clerk in name that lacks a cure,
> Whom idleness must needs ensnare in crime,
> Scandal — and worse — to screen an erring clerk,
> More fearing clamor than the cancer slow
> Of wily wasting sin. Scandal it is
> When seven rich benefices load one priest,
> Likeliest his soul's damnation.
> *John of Salisbury.* . Scandals indeed!
> And no true friend to Thomas is the man,
> Who palliates such abuses. For this cause
> Reluctantly he grasped Augustine's staff,
> Therewith to smite them down. Madam, the men
> Who brand them most are those who breed the scandals.
> The Primate warred on such. The King to shield them,
> Invoked the Royal Customs.

De Vere does not whiten the courtiers and sycophants, although clothed with episcopal authority, who shrank from St. Thomas at the King's scowl. He is even more pitiless to them than Tennyson. Tennyson, however, does not seem to see the anomaly of making an archbishop show an insubordinate and mutinous spirit, which almost justifies the hot words that King Henry is made to address to him:

> No! God forbid, and turn me Mussulman!
> No God but one, and Mahound is his prophet.
> But for your Christian, look you, you shall have
> None other God but me — me, Thomas, son
> Of Gilbert Becket, London merchant.

It may be said that Tennyson's idea of St. Thomas is very human, and that the poet has well depicted in rushing words a proud nature towering and neither bending nor breaking. It is well enough painted from that point of view. There are some exquisitely fine natural touches. But the poet-laureate had no right to attempt to depict the character of St. Thomas merely from that point of view. Pride and enthusiasm would never have made a Christian martyr of Thomas à Becket, and it is the full understanding of this that, leaving out other qualities, makes De Vere the greater poet and truer delineator of a hero whom it is almost sacrilege to misrepresent for the sake of a theatrical *succès d'estime*.

The character of Thomas à Becket belongs to Christendom and to history, and the poet-laureate, rushing in where angels fear to tread, not caring for or understanding the sacredness of his subject, did both Christendom and art a wrong by dragging an effigy of the martyred Primate in the dust. It used to be the fashion to overlook the liberties that poets and romance-writers took with history; but since historians have become romancers, and even adopted the adjectives of the poets, we are more exacting. No excuse can be offered for Tennyson's falsification of the character of À Becket, — so unlike that of Shakespeare's treatment of Wolsey, — not even an excuse that he needed dramatic color. He had a noble figure and a sublime time, and he belittled them both, because he would not understand them, or because he was desirous of the applause of the frequenters of theatres.

Tennyson causes the Pope's almoner to suggest treachery to the Archbishop when the King is urging him to sign the articles against the freedom of the Church. Philip de Eleemosyna tempts the Archbishop by whispering that the Pope wants him to do it:

> Cannot the Pope absolve thee if thou sign?

What plea can be offered for it in the careful, overwrought work of a poet whose fame is world-wide and whose sympathy should not have been much narrower?

Becket bursts out in this speech:

> Map scoffs at Rome. I all but hold with Map.
> Save for myself, no Rome were left in England:
> All had been his. Why should this Rome, this Rome,
> Still choose Barabbas rather than the Christ,
> Absolve the left-hand thief and damn the right?
> Take fees of tyranny, wink at sacrilege,
> Which even Peter had not dared? condemn
> The blameless exile?

Herbert of Bosham, the Archbishop's faithful friend, a devout cleric and a sensible man, is made to drivel:

> Thee, thou holy Thomas,
> I would that thou hadst been the Holy Father.

To which Tennyson's Archbishop complacently replies:

> I would have done my most to keep Rome holy:
> I would have made Rome know she still is Rome,
> Who stands aghast at her eternal self
> And shakes at mortal kings —

Chronicles tell us that St. Thomas was serene and dignified in all trials, but "Becket's" serenity is frequently swept away in gusts of evil temper, and he is quite as foul-mouthed as the enemies that bait him. The prelates around him wrangle like school-boys, and the scene at Northampton is simply a free quarrel. De Vere comprehending that the key to St. Thomas's conduct must be found in a supernatural motive, avoids the almost brutal mistakes of the laureate. The scene of the signing of the Royal Customs by À Becket was really at Clarendon; Tennyson transfers it to Roehampton. De Vere treats this scene with keen perception and admirable reticence. The Archbishop does not forget himself or burst into violent assertions. He is made to explain the episode of the almoner, which Tennyson treats in a very different way. He tells how he was deluded into signing the articles. It is very different from the version in which the Pope's envoy whispers that one may sin freely and be sure of absolution.

Came next the papal envoy from Aumone,
With word the Pope, moved by the troublous time,
Willed my submission to the royal will.
This was the second fraud; remains the third.
My lords, the Customs named till then were few.
In evil hour I yielded — pledged the Church,
Alas! to what I know not. On the instant
The King commanded, "Write ye down these laws,"
And soon, too soon, a parchment pre-ordained
Upon our table lay, a scroll inscribed
With usages sixteen, whereof most part
Were shamefuller than the worse discussed till then.
My lords, too late I read that scroll. I spurned it;
I swore by Him who made the heavens and earth
That never seal of mine should touch that bond,
Not mine, but juggle-changed. My lords, that eve
A truthful servant and a fearless one,
Who bears my cross, and taught me, too, to bear one, —
Llewellyn is his name, remembered be it! —
Probed me, and probed with sharp and searching words;
And as the sun my sin before me stood.
My lords for forty days I kept my fast,
And held me from the offering of the mass,
And sat in sackcloth; till the Pope sent word,
"Arise; be strong and walk!" And I arose,
And hither came; and here confession make
That till the cleansèd leper once again

> Take voluntary back his leprosy,
> I with those Royal Customs stain no more
> My soul, which Christ hath washed.

De Vere shows consummate skill in building up bit by bit the Archbishop, in accordance with the character given him by authentic writers. The Primate asked of his servants their honest opinions of this conduct, and accepted opinions thus frankly tendered as his guide. The flattery of Tennyson's Herbert of Bosham, so complacently swallowed by the laureate's political Primate, would have brought down the censure of the real St. Thomas.

De Vere characterizes Llewellyn, the Celtic cross-bearer, by a nice touch:

> The tables groaned with gold; I scorned the pageant;
> The Norman pirates and the Saxon boors
> Sat round and fed; I hated them alike,
> The rival races, one in sin. Alone
> We Britons tread our native soil.

Tennyson shows us the Archbishop rushing to his death from obstinacy and want of self-control. De Brito, Fitzurse, and De Tracy have come to put into act the hasty words of the King and to murder the Archbishop. Becket rails at them bitterly, throws Fitzurse from him, and pitches De Tracy "headlong" after the manner of the muscular Christian heroes beloved of the late Rev. Charles Kingsley. He even sneers at the monks whom Tennyson makes to flee. "Our dovecote flown!" he says, "I cannot tell why monks should all be cowards." He still repeats the sneer, until Grim, whose arm is broken by a blow aimed at Becket, reminds him that *he* is a monk. Rosamond rushes in and begs the murderers to spare the Archbishop, and then he is slain, just as a thunderstorm breaks. This climax, which in De Vere's tragedy follows strictly the authentic account of the sacrilege, is made trivial by a theatrical stroke.

There is nothing in Tennyson's "Becket" to compare with the lyrics in "The Princess," or even the lute song in "Queen Mary"; but they are airy and expressive of the mood of the persons in whose mouths they are placed. Queen Eleanor sings:

> Over! the sweet Summer closes,
>   The reign of roses is done;
> Over and gone with the roses,
>   And over and gone with the sun.

> Over ! the sweet Summer closes,
>   And never a flower at the close;
> Over and gone with the roses,
>   And Winter again and the snows.

It is quite in accordance with the mood of the light-minded Queen, who is quite past the August of life. She gives the impression that she was half-crazed, a kind of Provençal bacchante, and her first entrance destroys all respect for her sanity.

De Vere's "St. Thomas of Canterbury" has a contrast in "Becket" which makes it glow and seem more full of lustre and color, as a ruby put in a circle of brilliants. It is hard to account for the blindness of the poet of the "Idyls of the King" in venturing to attempt theatrically what had been already so well done. De Vere's place as a great poet was settled when "Alexander the Great" appeared. "St. Thomas of Canterbury" was not needed to teach the world what he could do. But he gave it out of the abundance of his heart; and we may thank God that we have a seer at once strong, pure, true to his ideals both in religion and art, worthy to wear the mantle that fell from the shoulders of Wordsworth.

But this fact remains: elevation of thought, force of poetry, fidelity to history, cannot make an acting play; so De Vere's tragedy is that anomalous thing, a "closet drama," and, really, with all its virtues, not a drama at all.

And this other fact, too, remains, that Tennyson, in attempting to be theatrical, left a form to which all the skill of Sir Henry Irving could not even give the shadow of dramatic vitality.

THE COMPARATIVE METHOD
  IN LITERATURE

THE COMPARATIVE METHOD IN LITERATURE

OF all critics Voltaire was the narrowest and the most incapable of appreciating the methods of comparative literature. He was almost ready to say, with LeClerc, "The English have many good books; it is a pity that the authors of that country can write only in their own language." And yet, narrow even to classical bigotry as he was, with regard to all literature that was not a French imitation of Greece and Rome, he admits the continuity, the relativity, the world-wide power of literature, when he says, "There are books that are like the fire on our hearths: we take a spark of this fire from our neighbors, we light our own with it; its warmth is communicated to others, and it belongs to all."

The business of the student of literature is to trace the pedigrees of books as well as to compare books with books. And this comparison, this power of tracing, implies in its result both concentration and expansion. Every book has its pedigree; and the ancestors of books, like the ancestors of persons, cannot be uprooted from the soil in which they grew; they are of their climate, of their time. As the bit of tapestry from a far-off Turkish palace carries the scent of the attar of roses to distant lands and through many changing years, so the book — one of a line of books — mingles with the current of thought long after it is forgotten, in the life of an alien nation. Joseph Texte, in his "Études de Littérature Européenne," says:

"A literature, no more than an animal organism, grows isolated from neighboring nations and literatures. The study of a living being is in a great part the study of the influences which unite it to beings near it and of the influences of all species which surround us like an invisible network. There is no literature, and perhaps no writer, of whom it can be said that the history confines itself within the limits of his own country. How can the evolution of German literature be understood, without knowing the reasons for the acceptance on the part of

German writers of the French influence, and then of its rejection for the English influence? The history of the influence of Shakespeare in Europe would, of itself, be an essential chapter in the history of modern literature. Romanticism is primarily an international event, which can be explained, as George Brandes says, only by the inter-relations of various literatures."

The sentimental romanticism of Goethe, as evident in "The Sorrows of Werther," is due to the same influence that made "La Nouvelle Héloïse" of Rousseau, and made Sterne's "The Sentimental Journey"; but before Rousseau we find that other sentimentalist, the Abbé Prévost, whose "Manon Lescaut" was the predecessor of "Paul and Virginia." Voltaire, as everybody knows, owed much of his worst quality to the English Bolingbroke. In his serious works we find English deism served with the *esprit Gaulois;* in the others, where wit and bitter cynicism play like infernal lightning, we find Rabelais changed, and yet the same. To quote from Joseph Texte again:

"It seems, finally, that the literature of the modern epoch — and perhaps of all epochs —

neither develops nor progressés without imitating or borrowing: imitation of antique, as in France in the seventeenth century; borrowing from neighboring literatures, as in Germany in the eighteenth. It is necessary, in order to make original works germinate, to prepare the soil with the débris of other works."

The student of literature, then, ought not to attempt to take one book and isolate it from its fellows. The beauty and freshness and humor of Chaucer may be enjoyed whether we go back to the trouvères for the sources of his earlier works, or trace the effects of Dante and Petrarch on those later in life; but for the broadening of the mind, for the perception of that sense of continuity so necessary for the knowledge of God's guidance in history, for the value of literature as a method of discovering the meaning of laws, it is well that Chaucer should be studied as a link in a chain. And yet not only as a link in a chain, but as a link in a chain running, as it were, through a closely knit coat of mail, touching and binding a hundred other links, large and small, without which the glittering garment of knighthood would be incomplete.

It deepens pleasure to know the relations of books to one another. It makes the study of literature easier, for it softens that feeling of desperation which strikes the reader when he enters a teeming library. Where shall he begin? How shall he hew a line through this wilderness of books? The genealogy of the book he loves will help him to do this, and its posterity will further assist in the work. Further, to put the study of the pedigrees of books on higher ground, who speaks the word "comparison," with the object of discovering truths, speaks the word "science." As Joseph Texte remarks:

"If the history of literature does not constitute an end in itself; if it aims, like all researches worthy of the name of science, at certain results which are at present beyond it; if it assumes, in fine, to be a form of the psychology of races and men, the comparative method imposes upon it the necessity of regarding the study of one type of men, or of one literature, as only an approach to a study more worthy to be called scientific."

There are many reasons, then, why books should be studied comparatively.

The mere investigation as to whether one book is an imitation of another is not so important or vital as the analysis of beauties that have stimulated greater beauties in another book. No reader will say that Plutarch and Shakespeare resemble each other. The Greek was a prose narrator, greatest in his way; the Englishman was a dramatic poet, greatest in his way; and yet the influence of Plutarch on "Julius Cæsar" and "Coriolanus" is unmistakable. It is as plain as the influence of the Byzantines on Giotto, or that of Wagner on the later manner of Verdi, or of Pindar on the English ode of the eighteenth century. Mangan and Poe seem to have no close relationship. As a rule, we do not think of them together, and yet it is difficult, after reading these poets, who evidently held peculiar and sensuous theories about poetry, to believe that Poe did not consciously imitate Mangan. And the German influences on Mangan are easily traced. How much Gaelic metres affected him, it is not, unfortunately, possible for me to say.

To return to Shakespeare: I once asked a friend of mine who loved only a few books, why he kept the maxims of Epictetus, the Roman slave, so near the plays of Shakespeare, who was more than any Roman patrician. He simply turned to a line out of Hamlet: " For there is nothing either good or bad, but thinking makes it so." " That is from Epictetus," he said, " and the more I study Shakespeare's philosophy, the more I find Epictetus." So the little volume held its place beside the many books of Shakespeare's plays, and further examination convinced me that it had reason to be there.

Emerson, to come from the reigns of Nero and Elizabeth to our own time, owes much to Epictetus, but more to Plato and Montaigne. He was not an imitator but an assimilator; to his philosophy we owe little, but to his power of stimulating idealism, much. Emerson reflects Plato and ·Montaigne and his New England skies at the same time. His Plato is not the Plato of the groves and the white temples, but Plato touched by the utilitarianism of the cotton factory; his Montaigne is not the gay and polite and witty and pensive Montaigne, content with his books and his Burgundy, but a restless Montaigne, frost-bitten by Puritanism, become oracular because his auditors were too busy to contradict him.

If you compare the four essays on "Friendship," — Cicero's, Montaigne's, Bacon's, Emerson's, — you will find the man Emerson surrounded and affected by the shades of his literary ancestors. If you examine his bumps, after the manner of the discredited practices of phrenology, you will find that they are all of the American type; but you will find, too, that the influence of his literary ancestors has, in its old-worldly way, corrected the indications which the bumps show. He is composite; and the study of the types that enter into his make-up will give a clue to the methods that ought to be used in the comparative study of other authors, who are all composite.

Voltaire says that nearly everything in literature is the result of imitation. But Voltaire was as deficient in desire and the power of real comparison as any of the Romans or Greeks. He was the slave of conventions; and was almost as rigid as that literary *sans culotte* who, in 1794, refused to save a victim from the guillotine because his petition had not been put into academic language! If Voltaire had said that everything great in literature was largely the result of assimilation, he would have been much nearer the truth. There are those who call Tennyson classical, in the sense of coldness and symmetry; yet it can be easily shown that one of his most influential literary ancestors was Byron, who can be called neither cold nor classical. In fact, if any poet is romantic, and sentimentally romantic, Byron is that poet. In "Locksley Hall" and "Maud," there is the Byronic note, without the depths of Byronic despair. In the first part of "Locksley Hall" Tennyson's hopes and ideals are infinitely higher than Byron's, and the passion is infinitely purer in "Maud." In the second part of "Locksley Hall" the impetuous boy, who feels that the world had come to an end when Byron died, has disappeared in the old man, whose hopes in the "Christ to come" through science and the new social order have completely gone out. Tennyson's poetry has a long pedigree; and there are many quarterings on its coat of arms: among the heraldic colors is the vert of Wordsworth as well as the flaring vermilion of Byron; but there is one especially that cannot be expressed by any feudal tinct, and another that may be symbolized by many. The first is Theocritus; the second, Sir Thomas Malory.

From the first, Tennyson borrowed the title of the greatest of modern epics, "The Idyls of the King." And the influence of Theocritus, the sweetest of all pastoral singers, is found everywhere, but most of all in "Œnone." Theocritus, who was an ancestor of Vergil and of all later pastoral poets, takes new life in Tennyson. Even the English verse translations of this singer of the reed and the cypress and of the contest of the shepherds in the green pastures cannot wholly shut his beauty from our view. It is as hard to endure his artificial image as set up by Pope as it is to endure that of Chaucer as regilded by Dryden. Even Mrs. Browning handles his exquisite idyls with a touch that does not fit the violet of the Spring. In prose translations some of the aroma escapes, but enough of it remains to cheer the soul with loveliness. To read him in youth is never to forget him. For Theocritus was the poet of nature, the inventor of the little idyl-pictures of town or country,— that singer of idyls who, nearly three hundred years before Christ, saw dimly Nature's God. He says in the seventh *eidulla:*

"And from above, down upon our heads were waving to and fro many poplars and elms; and the sacred stream hard by kept murmuring, as it flowed down from the cave of the nymphs. And the fire-colored cicalas, on the shady branches, were toiling at chirping; while, from afar off, in the thick thorn-bushes the thrush was warbling. Tufted larks and goldfinches sang, the turtle-dove cooed; tawny bees were humming round the fountains; all things were breathing the incense of very plenteous Summer and of fruit-time. Pears fell at our feet, and apples were rolling for us in abundance, and the boughs hung in profusion, weighed down to the ground with plums."

The warmth of the Summer is in Theocritus. The gold and purple bees float in the dry down of the thistle, and Demeter's symbols, the spikes of corn and poppies, glow golden and scarlet in the soft Sicilian air. Tennyson, too, gives the color of the Summer and the incense of the Autumn in symbols suggested by the Syracusan. And from the refrains of Theocritus he borrows, as Poe borrows from Mangan, the cadence of his music.

Edmund Clarence Stedman, in "The Victorian Poets," has some pregnant chapters on the resemblance of Theocritus and Tennyson, and his passages showing how Theocritus vitalized the English poet as a bee vitalizes a flower are culled with exquisite insight and taste. Among these Mr. Stedman quotes the delicious appeal of Cyclops to Galatea (in the Eleventh Idyl), to compare it with the passage in Book VII of "The Princess":

Come down, O maid, from yonder mountain height:
What pleasure lives in height (the shepherd sang),
In height and cold, the splendor of the hills?

There is the echo of the Sicilian Summer in "The Gardener's Daughter":

All the land in flowery squares,
Beneath a broad and equal-blowing wind,
Smelt of the coming Summer. . . .

>   From the woods
> Came voices of the well-contented doves.
> The lark could scarce get out his notes for joy,
> But shook his song together as he near'd
> His happy home, the ground. To left and right,
> The cuckoo told his name to all the hills;
> The mellow ouzel fluted in the elm;
> The redcap whistled; and the nightingale
> Sang loud, a though he were a bird of day.

"Œnone," with the pathetic refrain suggested by both Theocritus and Moschus, could not have existed in its present form, had not the Syracusan sung amid the hyacinth and arbutus.

In the black-letter of Sir Thomas Malory, Tennyson read many times, until his mind and heart were steeped in the wonder of the old stories; and from the Elizabethan poets, who had learned much from their Italian brethren, he borrowed the allegory and added it to the tales of Sir Thomas. Spenser himself, following Ariosto, — for Ariosto is the chief literary ancestor of Spenser, — had made an allegory. Tennyson strung the many-colored gems of Sir Thomas on the silver string of his veiled meaning. Or rather, as he told his tales, the beads of his allegory slipped through his fingers. But the stories of the knights were greatly changed by the modern poet. Arthur is not, in "The Idyls of the King," the terrible monarch of fire and blood of Sir Thomas Malory. Another age and other manners have softened the chivalric compromises of the earlier times, for chivalry seems to have been a series of compromises with an ideal in the distance. The Arthur of Sir Thomas Malory is not the saintly King of Tennyson's imagination. In Malory's "Morte Arthure," he does and says things very inconsistent with the ideal blameless King we love and revere in the "Idyls." And the allegory which Tennyson wove cannot be read into the rough doings of Arthur's knights. Nor did Sir Thomas, or the sympathetic Caxton who printed his book, see things as Spenser and Milton and Tennyson saw them, — all these seeing differently according to the light of their time. But, if a book may be judged by its effects, the "Morte Arthure" does not deserve the condemnation of those Elizabethan Reformers, like Roger Ascham, who could excuse murder and adultery in an unrepentant real king, but held up hands of horror at a mythical one, even when he repented. Says the grand old printer, Caxton, in his preface to the "Morte Arthure":

"Herein may be seen noble chivalry, courtesy, humanity, friendlessness, hardiness, love, friendship, cowardice, murder, hate, virtue, sin. All is written for our doctrine, for to beware that we fall not into vice or sin, but to exercise and follow virtue, by which we may come and attain to good fame and renommee in this life, and after this to come unto everlasting bliss in Heaven; the which He grants us that reigneth in heaven, the Blessed Trinity. Amen.

"'Ah, my Lord Arthur,' cries Sir Bedevere, on the last day of the fight, 'what shall become of me now ye go from me and leave me here alone among my enemies?' 'Comfort thyself,' said the King, 'and do as well as thou mayest, for in me is no trust for to trust in. For I will unto the vale of Avilion to heal me of my grievous wound. And if thou hear never more of me, pray for my soul!'"

We can all recall the Homeric echo of this in Tennyson's —

The old order changeth, yielding place to new,
And God fulfils himself in many ways,
Lest one good custom should corrupt the world.

Comfort thyself; what comfort is in me?
I have lived my life, and that which I have done
May He within himself make pure! but thou
If thou shouldst never see my face again,
Pray for my soul. More things are wrought by prayer
Than this world dreams of. Wherefore, let thy voice
Rise like a fountain for me night and day.
For what are men better than sheep or goats
That nourish a blind life within the brain,
If, knowing God, they lift not hands of prayer
Both for themselves and those who call them friend?
For so the whole round earth is every way
Bound by gold chains about the feet of God.

"Now," says old Sir Thomas, when the roses have faded, "now we leave Guinever in Almsbury a nun in white and black, and there she was abbess and ruler, as reason would." How Tennyson refines upon this in the light of more cultured genius and finer days! You remember the simple little novice who sits at the sad Queen's feet, and sings:

Too late, too late, ye cannot enter now!

Tennyson writes of the nuns and Guinevere:

They took her to themselves; and she
Still hoping, fearing, "Is it yet too late?"
Dwelt with them, till in time their abbess died.

Then she, for her good deeds and her pure life,
And for the power of ministration in her,
And likewise for the high rank she had borne,
Was chosen abbess, there, an abbess, lived
For three brief years, and there, an abbess pass'd
To where beyond these voices there is peace.

It is the province of genius, as Emerson says, to borrow nobly. If the immediate ancestor of "The Idyls of the King" was the "Morte Arthure" as to matter, the remote ancestor was the "Idyls" of Theocritus as to form and manner. But I think it needs only time to show how many other prose writers and poets, how many changes of philosophies, customs, and points of view, it takes to make any writer who speaks to the soul with wisdom and to the heart with beauty. A poet descends from heaven, step by step, like Jacob's angels on bars of celestial light. God only can create him, and the Ancient of Days makes every hour from the beginning move toward his coming,—and each poet is the father of another poet.

Tennyson was the child of Sir Thomas Malory and of his own time, as Dante was of Vergil and of his time; as Milton was of the Old Testament as interpreted by the rebels of his time; as William Morris was of Chaucer, accentuated by the tense romanticism of Dante Rossetti and the early Provençal poets.

Theocritus, Sir Thomas Malory, Tennyson! How near, and yet how far apart! And comparatively, how many allied shades they recall! You mention "The Holy Grail," and up rise Spenser, Milton, Lowell,— the Lowell of Sir Launfal, — and then Wagner's "Parsifal," and spirit of beauty after spirit of beauty, until the earliest of them seems to touch the very seraphim. We can as easily leave out St. Thomas and St. Francis of Assisi in considering the genesis of Dante as we can consider any modern great work of literature without reference to its pedigree. Music, too, is closely bound to literature, — the myth of Lohengrin is only a later version of that of Cupid and Psyche. Wagner could not have done what he did without the Niebelungenlied; nor Gounod, if the Middle Age legend of Faust had not been told from mouth to mouth, until

Goethe, borrowing nobly from the Book of Job, made Faust vital and grandiose for all time. If culture means the broadening of the mind through the widest knowledge of the best, it is hard to see with what reason we can neglect the study of the pedigrees of books.

If Tennyson succeeded Wordsworth, Tennyson also succeeded Byron. While Wordsworth was serene, a painter of nature, Byron was the opposite of him. He was fiery, volcanic, furious, lurid, great in genius. He was popular, while Wordsworth, whom the world is now only beginning to acknowledge, was neglected; so that, strange as it may seem at first, Tennyson's immediate predecessor was Lord Byron. Byron's popularity was great while he lived. The hero of "Locksley Hall" — I mean the first part of it, for I think the second part is decidedly the better — is a Byronic hero diluted. And the hero of "Maud" is of a similar type.

In "Locksley Hall" the hero sighs and moans and calls Heaven's vengeance down on his ancestral roof because a girl has refused to marry him; because his cousin Amy marries another man, he goes into a paroxysm of poetry and denunciation and prophecy. But, as Shakespeare says, "Men have died from time to time and worms have eaten them, but not for love." And the hero of "Locksley Hall" lives to write in a calmer style a good many years later. "Maud," like "Locksley Hall," showed something of the influence of Byron. After "Locksley Hall" and "Maud," the effect of Byron on Tennyson seems to grow less.

The young Tennyson's favorite poet was Thomson, he of the serene and gentle "Seasons." Mrs. Ritchie tells us how very early the influence of Thomson showed itself:

"Alfred's first verses, so I have heard him say, were written upon a slate which his brother Charles put into his hand one Sunday at Louth, when all the elders of the party were going into church and the child was left alone. Charles gave him a subject,— the flowers in the garden, —and when he came back from church little Alfred brought the slate to his brother, all covered with written lines of blank verse. They were made on the model of Thomson's "Seasons," the only poetry he had ever read,

One can picture it all to oneself, the flowers in the garden, the verses, the little poet with waiting eyes, and the young brother scanning the lines. 'Yes, you can write,' said Charles, and he gave Alfred back the slate."

The poet of Alfred's first love was the calm and pleasant Thomson, we see. Later, as he grew toward manhood, he read Byron. He scribbled in the Byronic strain. How strong a hold Byron's fiery verse had taken on the boy's mind is shown by his own confession. When Alfred was about fifteen, the news came that Byron was dead. "I thought the whole world was at an end," he said. "I thought everything was over and finished for everyone — that nothing else mattered. I remember I walked out alone, and carved ' Byron is dead' into the sandstone." Although "Locksley Hall" and "Maud" show Byronic reflections, yet they were not the earliest published of Tennyson's poems.

The Greek poet, Moschus, wrote an elegy on his friend Bion, and the refrain of this elegy, "Begin, Sicilian muses, begin the lament," is famous. Tennyson, this modern poet, possessed of the Greek passion for symmetry, and influenced almost as much by Theocritus, Moschus, and Bion as by the spirit of his own time, has made an elegy on his friend as solemn, as stately, as perfect in its form as that of Moschus, but not so spontaneous and tender. There is more pathos in King David's few words over the body of Absalom than in all the noble falls and swells of "In Memoriam."

I doubt whether any heart in affliction has received genuine consolation from this decorous and superbly measured flow of grief. It is not a poem of faith, nor is it a poem of doubt; but faith and doubt tread upon each other's footsteps. Instead of the divine certitude of Dante, we have a doubting half-belief. Tennyson loves the village church, the holly-wreathed baptismal font, the peaceful vicarage, because they represent serenity and order. He detests revolution. If he had lived before the coming of Christ, in the vales of Sicily, he would probably have hated to see the rural sports of the pagans disturbed by the disciples of a less picturesque and less natural religion.

Keats could not have been Keats as we

know him, without Spenser. He is called Greek, but he knew Greek best through Chapman's Homer. Yet he caught the spirit, and the form for him did not matter, — he had that from the "Epithalamium" of Spenser; and "no poet," as M. Texte admits, "has excited more vocations to poetry than Spenser." He is, like Shelley, the poet for the poet. Other poets may speak to the world; he sings to the sacred city. He lacks the elevation of Spenser, deflected as it was by the Elizabethan concession to the political spirit of his time; he is without the unconsciousness of the Greeks, whose spirit he assumed without understanding it. He longed for sensations rather than thoughts, for dreams rather than activities. He was romantic, if romance implies aspiration. The "Ode to the Nightingale" expresses Keats. He was half in love with "easeful death." He was not Greek in this; his neohellenism is like the paganism of Swinburne, — it cannot rid itself of the shadow of the Cross; it is black against the light of the Resurrection. Like Maurice de Guérin, he loved the pleasures of sensation, and the fact that they must pass filled him with fear. He turns to the immortal figures on the Grecian urn with wild regret; — all in life that has life, dies; only the work of the artist, who uses inorganic stuff for his material, lives! He felt, indeed, that his name was writ in water before Shelley made that splendid epitaph.

"Endymion" is a poem of shadows in the moonlight. It is not Greek, but it is touched by the spirit of Greece. It is romantic because it bears everywhere the burden of the poet's longing. "A joy forever" he longs for; but all joys pass as the moon passes, and the shades of beauty with it. Keats is a neo-Grecian, if you will; his literary ancestors are the gods of the rivers and the woods, as Greek singers made them; but he is nearer to Ovid than to Theocritus, nearer to Vergil than to Bion, and nearest of all to this time, which, under the influence of Sir Walter Scott and Byron, was the time of longing for light and color and glow and beauty that should be eternal. He, in his turn, had influenced many. When we speak of the Preraphaelites, we imply the name of Keats. "The

Earthly Paradise" of William Morris presumes the influence of Chaucer; but who can read from "The Earthly Paradise" without thinking of Keats?

> Of Heaven or Hell I have no power to sing,
> I cannot ease the burden of your fears,
> Or make quick-coming death a little thing,
> Or bring again the pleasure of past years,
> Nor for my words shall ye forget your tears,
> Or hope again for aught that I can say,
> The idle singer of an empty day.

What we call the Puritanism of Spenser was, on its spiritual side, the eclipsed light of the Catholic years that had passed; it sustained him, for he was the son of Ariosto and of truth and beauty. And the Puritanism of Milton,— of the mind, not of the heart,— while it vitiated his Christianity, did not subdue his Hebraic elevation. Keats, the poet of earthly beauty, had the feeling of the Greek for the sensations of life, but he was oppressed by the fear that a day would come when he and life must part. Heine, a great lyrist, too (he was Greek by turns, less sublimated than Keats), stood old, almost blind, paralyzed, at the foot of the statue of Venus of Melos, in the Louvre.

And the world seemed about to go to pieces, for the Revolution of 1848 roared around him. The true Greek would have died, satisfied that he had lived his life. But Heine, who had lived for earthly beauty and joy, who was already dead because the pleasures of life were dead to him, cried aloud in despair. Earth could not give immortality! Of these neo-Greeks — not of the old Greeks, but touched by their spirit — was Keats.

The elegy of Theocritus for Daphnis has echoed ever since he called on the Sicilian muses to weep with him. If it, with the recurrent refrain of musical sorrow, touched Tennyson in our time to sing of the dead Hallam, it spurred Milton to raise the voice of music over Lycidas, and Shelley to consecrate the immortal "Adonais" to Keats. The pedigree of the English elegy is as easily traced as that of the English ode, with whose richness our literature actually blazes. The Pindaric ode is a name of horror in English, since a slavish imitation of the sublime Greek distorted some of the finest odes of Gray and Collins. The spirit of Pindar helped to make the English ode the most beautiful in all the world, but the attempt to give Greek form to our verse has almost ruined, by meaningless strophes and antistrophes, some of the loveliest of English odes. I need only indicate the pedigree of the ode at the highest by mentioning three sublime names, — St. Teresa, Crashaw, Coventry Patmore.

The raptures of St. Teresa inspired Crashaw with the ode beginning —

> Love, thou art absolute sole lord
> Of life and death,

and with that other ode, less dignified because its form is an English imitation of the exquisite ever-changing music of Pindar, which can be transmitted into our tongue only by interpretation. Pindar influences the form, and St. Teresa the spirit; but Patmore is touched by Crashaw and not at all by the form of Pindar, though he is nearer to Pindar than any other of the poets, who failed to see that each of his odes had a delicate shell-like music of its own which could not be expressed by a short jumping line thrown in here and there among the longer ones. William Sharp says:

"Each of the odes of Pindar has its own music, as each conch stranded by the waves has its own forlorn vibration of the sea's rhythm; whereas the so-called Pindaric odes of Cowley and his imitators have no more individuality of music than have the exercises of instrumentalists in contradistinction to the compositions of musicians."

The pedigree of the Pindaric ode in English offers an admirable subject for the study of a beautiful form twisted into an incongruous shape by poets who blindly followed one another.

There can be no question that a comparative study of the literature of the Japanese and the Italian, the Basque and the Teuton, would make for cosmopolitanism, but who can speak of fixed literary laws which shall bear exact scientific analysis, without stretching the word "literary" so thin that it must break? Philosophy may be cosmopolitan or international — Christianity is universal; and if the whole world were Christendom, animated and active, there would be only one spirit in literature; but literature of itself must, until the world shall all be one way of thinking and feeling, be as varied as Milton's leaves in Vallombrosa; for no two leaves are exactly alike, though they are all leaves.

Still, the value and beauty of literature are best studied by processes of comparison which may be called scientific, and these processes of comparison are rendered easier by the consideration of the pedigrees of books.

A DEFINITION OF LITERATURE

A DEFINITION OF LITERATURE

IT is very hard to find even a working definition of literature. Literature is so closely the expression of life and the changing conditions of life that we can hardly limit it except by life itself. And a working definition must have limitations, though it may not entirely cover the thing intended to be defined. To the Greeks of Athens and the Romans of the city of Augustus, it meant the imitation of elegant models; to us it means the expression of the phenomena of life in the form of written words.

We can understand the meaning of literature only by studying the effects of ethical, social, political movements upon life; and this is best done through the literatures of peoples, subject to their changes. The body of Hebrew literature, through which God himself has spoken, is the history of the Jewish people. If it were merely the clear dry annals of the Jewish people, it would be history, not literature. But when we find the minds of David and Job revealed in words, we have essential history, but something more than a mere annal, which is not literature.

Literature, as far as it can be described to-day, is more than the reflection of life; and it is much more than it seemed to be to the Athenian Greeks, the Augustan Romans, the French of the time of Richelieu, or the Italians of the Renaissance; for, in their eyes, it was a narrow thing, capable of rigid definition. It was not what they imagined it to be, and they — as the " Poetics " of Aristotle and its imitations show us — did not really succeed in defining it. It was always elusive, in spite of their fine rhetorical terms. They pursued it, as Apollo pursued Daphne, only to find, when they came near, that the nymph had turned into a bay tree. To them literature was a Galatea, who by all the rules should have been marble, but who under the very eyes of the critic amazed him by assuming the life and incomprehensible fantasies of the universal woman.

Literature in general, when we attempt to define it, becomes as elusive as the highest of its forms, which is poetry. Literature reflects life in all its phases, to use a trite comparison, as some of the old Gothic cathedrals reflect life — from the agonizing figure on the rood screen to the grinning gargoyles on the roof and the vile little demons — the seven deadly sins — carved on the backs of the remote stalls. It has its spires that spring up as high as the clouds, and its crawling things of the earth, symbolical of the vices of the people that produce it. Its form changes, not only with every great impulse of force, but with every slight change of emotion. It expresses, it illuminates, it interprets; it cannot exist without thought, but it is more than thought. It is not philosophy, but it is impregnated with the effects of philosophy. It is not logic, or metaphysics, or ethics; but it cannot exist in perfection without a logical basis — and it partakes of metaphysics and ethics. It is neither scientia in the old sense — for pure and colorless truth cannot be literature — nor science in the new; yet it exists through truth, and its phenomena are best explained by the methods of science. It is not history, yet it is the beginning of history. It is not the personal word alone, yet the personal word is necessary to its existence. As I said, it is not ethics, yet it expresses the morality of the nation whose life it interprets. It is minutely personal — personality is one of its essences, and yet it represents better than anything else the national life.

It has made war and restored peace; it has raised men to the shining feet of God and led them to hell "to the lascivious pulsings of the lute." Dryden, in "Alexander's Feast," manifests the power of music, but it was not music alone that appealed to the great Alexander; it was literature allied to music, — the soul of the body.

The definitions of literature are as numerous and as inadequate as those offered for poetry; and they have given rise to as many misunderstandings. These misunderstandings have induced certain modern scientists to scorn literature as lawless, and yet to assume the language of literature to express their jibes, — not always to assume it with grace, but, at any rate, to use it, in order to be heard by all. These jeering scientists have this, at least, in common with the God they doubt, — that they, unconsciously imitating Him, took the form of literature when they spoke to man. And the more literary they are, the more the world heeds them. These misunderstandings once led that most methodical and scientific man of letters, Ferdinand Brunetière, to assert that science is bankrupt; it has enormous assets, — assets so great that it need not apply to the theologians for the certification of its cheques. Its bad reputation is due entirely to the fact that certain of its stockholders have forced drafts on that great theological establishment which it can neither dominate nor destroy.

Literature is not, as Mr. Louis Stevenson once defined it, a mere *fille de joie*, to be enjoyed and cast aside, — a *ballade* for the ears of the banqueting prince, a precious *rondeau* for the languid lady in the balcony; literature is not, as Cardinal Newman implies, only the personal use of language; it is not, as Mr. Matthew Arnold would have us believe, the ethics of the philosophy of life; it is not, as

Mr. Swinburne insists, at its culmination only imagination and harmony.

In his " Comparative Literature " Professor Posnett says that works of literature, whether in verse or prose,

" are the handicraft of imagination rather than reflection, aim at the pleasure of the greatest number of the nation rather than instruction and practical effects, and appeal to general rather than specialized knowledge. . . . Every element of this definition clearly depends on the limited spheres of social and mental evolution — the separation of imagination from experience, of didactic purpose from æsthetic pleasure, and that specialization of knowledge which is so largely due to the economic development known as 'division of labor.' "

We shall, I am sure, all consent to the assertion that the value of literature must be sought for in inherent personal qualities, and its source must be looked for in human nature rather than in artful rules gathered from the examination of classic books. We are sure, too, that the maxims of Aristotle — those, I mean, which are not founded on human nature's love of contrast, hatred of monotony, and the desire to be taken out of the bounds of self — fail to indicate the scientific bases of literature because they force the material to suit the shape of the mould they impose. We have gone beyond the blind acceptance of the old standards to which the epic, the tragedy, and the lyric were forced to adjust themselves. It is as impossible to use them to-day as it is impossible to turn our uninflected English into genuine hexameters. On close comparison with the thing defined, Professor Posnett's definition proves as unsatisfactory as hitherto all definitions have proved.

Let us consider those manifestations of the life of the soul on which he founds this definition. However we may differ in opinion as to the relative value of other works of high literary art, there is only one opinion about Dante's "Inferno." You may argue about the "Purgatorio" or the "Paradiso," if you will. You may insist, too, that Milton's "Paradise Regained" is a failure; but you must admit the eminence of "Paradise Lost." No cultivated man will deny the masterly qualities of the first part of "Faust," though he may be reserved in his admiration of the second. It is agreed that the

"Inferno," "Paradise Lost," and the first part of "Faust" are noble works of literature. And it is plain that the object or the effect of these three masterpieces is not to give pleasure, — that higher pleasure of which even the Utilitarians admit the existence. The object of Dante was beyond and above the giving of pleasure. When Milton pondered and wrought until "dim suffusion" veiled his orbs, it was not to give pleasure to the greatest number. And who really believes that Keats, rapt in the vision of Diana and Endymion, spoke with the Utilitarian purpose? And who, knowing how Maurice de Guérin wrote "Le Centaure" for God, silence, and himself, can fail to see that some of the greatest things of literature owe their existence to the desire to express and yet not to communicate?

There are great poems, like Browning's "Sordello" and "The Ring and the Book," that are beyond the liking or understanding of the greatest number. If we leave out the author's intention and consider only the matter of effect, we find, in the so-called sonnets of Shakespeare, great literature so personal and yet so appealing that the interpreters far exceed in number those to whom its beauty clearly speaks. That flower of lyrical literature, the "Epithalamium" of Spenser, touches only the few. Admitting that the "Inferno" is literature, and leaving out the question as to whether it appeals to many or not, we cannot help seeing that Professor Posnett's definition does not touch it. I accentuate his definition because it is largely accepted, and because Professor Posnett assumes that it is scientific. It is evident that in the "Inferno" Dante aimed at "instruction and practical effects"; it is evident that he attained his object by illuminating his processes with imagination and harmony; and yet, if we accept this very modern definition, Dante and Milton must be exiled, as Plato would have exiled all the poets,— but for a different reason.

When Orlando carved the name of Rosalind on the bark of the oaks in the Forest of Arden, he felt the impulse of many poets, yet he made the name only for silence and himself. Literature cannot be judged as literature by the Utilitarian criterion. To make it a matter for the suffrage of the greatest number is to take it into the ground now occupied by politics. A literary man crowned by the universal suffrage of the American people — if the elect did not mercifully intimidate voters — would be, for all time, a pleasing example of mediocrity!

With the beginning of the new century the worship of Goethe has taken new vigor. On all sides ascend thick incense clouds to the manes of the many-sided. But why is Goethe acclaimed? Because of the æsthetic pleasure his lyrics give? Because of the purely romantic qualities of "Goetz" or the imaginative glow of "Faust"? Not at all, — though these qualities, too, are acclaimed, — but because in his works are said to be found the germs of modern scientific development. He is not regarded as less than a poet for this or less of a man of letters, but as more of a poet and more of a maker of literature. A great part of his claim on the modern mind rests, then, on the very qualities which Professor Posnett eliminates from literature. But Dante, the poet philosopher who expressed Aristotle and St. Thomas and all the science of his day, who founded the study of comparative philology, would not be lowered in the scale of literature if all his erudition were plucked from him. Erudition or science or experience is unpoetical only when the poet is too small for the weight he attempts to carry. But Dante was able to give harmony and the imaginative nimbus and symmetry and color to both abstractions and facts. There are poems great in themselves, which are all compact of harmony and imagination, — for example, Shelley's "Ode to the Skylark," Keats's "Grecian Urn," Lanier's "Centennial Ode," Patmore's "Ode to the Body." These may be covered by this definition; and still the mystical bases of the last of them, founded on philosophy and theology, come perilously near to ruling it out.

Permit me to repeat Professor Posnett's definition. It is found on page eighteen of his "Comparative Literature."[1] Literature consists "of works which, whether

---

[1] "Comparative Literature," by H. Macaulay Posnett. D. Appleton & Co., New York, 1896. "The Science of Comparative Literature," by H. Macaulay Posnett, *The Contemporary Review*, 1901.

in verse or prose, are the handicraft of imagination rather than reflection, aim at the pleasure of the greatest possible number of the nation rather than instruction and practical effects, and appeal to general rather than to specialized knowledge."

If we deny the value of this definition, how can literature be defined? I am not sure that the big word literature can be defined at all — I am not certain that the great and ever-changing subject it stands for will ever be rigidly described. But it seems to me that to-day literature is the expression in writing of thought, experience, observation, emotion, mood, knowledge personally expressed. Newman comes very near to this in his definition of style. Scientia, pure and simple, is not literature. There is no personal expression in the Apostles' Creed, though the personal pronoun is used for the will that accepts scientia. The Apostles' Creed is not literature; it belongs wholly to no one person; it is universal. The epical Isaiah, the pastoral Ruth, the lyrical David, are literature. And close are the relations of this literature to the spiritual life.

Darwin's book on the "Descent of Man" is literature, but not of the highest kind. Newman's "Grammar of Assent" is literature, but not of so high a kind as his more personal "Apologia." Tyndall's "Lectures" are literature, — more so, from the point of view of style than Herbert Spencer's. Froude's "History of England" is literature, differing from the two last-mentioned books because it is of the literature of fiction and because it is altogether finer in its expression. Lingard, on the contrary, made good history, but poor literature. The circle of science does not touch the circle of literature when science expresses itself impersonally, — anything personally expressed and not inconsistent with the genius of its language is literature; but the degrees of literature differ as the faintest nebulæ from the flashing constellations. This is as far as I can go in trying to describe literature.

But life is the pulse of literature, — literature marks the movements of the tendencies of life. It progresses as the individual progresses; it progresses as the nation progresses. And yet this progress, so far as the nation is concerned, has frequently ceased; it has ceased even before the death of the nation. The literature of a nation that has been great never dies. Plutarch and Seneca have influenced minds, Theocritus and Horace have influenced hearts, more than Cæsar or Augustus ever influences minds or hearts. Life has always turned toward God; and literature, echoing life, has always written the symbol of God. Life expressed by Æschylus is far from the life that made Racine as he was; life changing with Job is a far different life from the life that Faust loved; and yet from Cædmon to Milton, from Pindar's Odes to Wordsworth's "Intimations of Immortality," life turns to the First Cause. St. Augustine expresses His beauty; Dante, His splendor and justice; and Longfellow, drawn by that chain which binds genius to Him, shows His halo on the brow of faithful womanhood.

Life cannot escape from its Creator, and literature, pulsating with life, acknowledges His power. Leopardi, Carducci, Swinburne — fallen, clad, to use Ruskin's phrase, in "melancholy gold" — curse the flaming sword that will not allow Pan to come back to earth. Leopardi asks for death; Carducci and Swinburne yearn for the time before the Galilean had conquered. They express tendencies of life, not merely themselves. God, who is the centre of life, is the centre of the written expression of life, which is literature. St. Paul cries, with God in his heart: "Charity is patient, is kind; charity envieth not, dealeth not perversely, is not puffed up. . . . We see now through a glass in a dark manner; but then face to face. Now I know in part; but then I shall know even as I am known." St. Augustine begins a passage full of joy in God: "And thou gavest my mother another answer to her prayers, which I remember." All this, coming from the soul of life, is literature. If St. Thomas, in the "Hymns of the Blessed Sacrament" expresses scientia, his manner is exceedingly personal and literary. The theologian who pretends to despise literature, or to look upon it as a mere toy, as the Turks looked on woman, is likely to fall into the heresy of the Turks and to assume that his mother had no soul.

There can be no doubt that some of the misunderstandings of the relations of literature to life are due to the practitioners of literature themselves. They have claimed to be as mystically irresponsible as the Delphic oracle or the Howling Dervishes. Imagination — untrammelled imagination — was their idol. They pretended that they lived in flashes of divine fire, when, in fact, the clever had frequently caught them trying to strike damp matches upon mouldy "afflatuses." There were no laws for them; they sang as the wind sings; they were reeds by the river of the Ineffable. They gushed carefully written impromptus. Order, dignity, knowledge was valueless. And the more ignorant of the cultured took these gentlemen at their own valuation. And hence arose legends of the mad, glad, bad poet. And he warmed his hands by the divine fire in his cold garret. And he had no food but a roast leg of Pegasus served with laurel leaves boiled by the muses. And there was not any such person. And so they called him a Bohemian!

There have been, too, enthusiastic apologists who could not see that the great author and the little author were bound by the conditions of ordinary life. Literature, they have said, — literature that comes from great minds, — is universal. Its producer knows all things by intuition. But Dante was a hard student; still, there were many things he did not know. Coleridge, like a priest of Isis, gashed himself, to adore Shakespeare. The Bard of Avon was all-knowing, of all time — intuition made him so. Law! — gods, what a lawyer he was! Philosopher! — he must have been, in dreams, intimate with the Greeks! Zoölogist! — how wonderful! In spite of Coleridge, lawyers have shown how superficial was Shakespeare's knowledge of law. It is evident that he was so ignorant of the facts of animal life, beyond Warwickshire, that he might have written Goldsmith's "Animated Nature." What he saw — and he knew how to see — he expressed. He was not above life or law or the conditions of life. He was of his time; his local prejudices and points of view limited him. His power of synthesis was great, but he cultivated it from his youth up. He was no more all-knowing than Dante, or Calderon, or Goethe, or Wordsworth was all-knowing.

On the other hand, in English-speaking countries, which are the last to realize what art means, literature has not been approached rationally, as Matthew Arnold scornfully admits. The man who had lately acquired much from the Germans without in the least understanding it laughed loftily at literature because he had discovered a new worm. Dante might sing of the seraphim, but your scientist of this sort doubted the existence of seraphim because, as there was no record of their vaccination, they must have died of small-pox! Mere philosophy he might accept; anybody of ordinary intelligence could count combinations of vowels, and it was even possible that the catarrh prevalent in the lake districts might have effected the consonantal sounds. These gentlemen would have sacrificed the Book of Job for a new principle of motion, and the Iliad for the discovery of the jumping apparatus in the skeleton of a flea. A new earth had come, without a new heaven, — romance and poetry and lyrical beauty had gone. Literature and science had met, and science had conquered, leaving

>A broken chancel with a broken cross.

Of course this was irrational. The only man of letters who took this sort of thing seriously was Zola. He tried to turn himself into a scientific naturalist; he became a creature so monstrous that even curiosity became disgusted.

There can be no conflict between literature and science. There could be no conquering of one by the other, nor driving of one by the other out of its proper domain, unless the longing to draw nearer the immortal, the love of harmony, the interest in other lives, the desire for the ideal, the yearning for a broader and a better life were taken from our existence here; for literature, the production of life, answers to the burning needs of life.

Lowell says that fairy tales, consolations in the twilight of desolation, are "the dreams of the poor." Science could analyze Puck and prove him to be wandering phosphorus, and that the spectres of

Rip Van Winkle in the Catskills were due to microbes in his whiskey. Science, for a time, — being young and ignorant, but not intrinsically evil, — seemed to forget that humanity loves the fairies of its dreams, not because they exist, but because it wants them to exist. It was a phase of life that science should have attacked, and not literature, which merely presented this phase.

Literature, rationally studied, will be found to touch life at all points. It does not always concern itself with the dreams of those who dwell in exile. It does not always concern itself with ideals. " Man's work," Newman says, in " The Idea of a University," " will savor of man, in his element and power excellent and admirable, but prone to disorder and excess, to error and to sin. Such, too, will be his literature; it will have the beauty and the fierceness, the sweetness and the rankness, of the natural man, and, with all its richness and greatness, it will necessarily offend the senses of those who, in the Apostle's words, are really ' exercised to the discerning of good and evil.' "

This is true, for literature is like the string of a violin in tune; it responds to the slightest change of national temperature. It was aristocratic and classical under Augustus and Louis XIV; aristocratic and romantic under Elizabeth. It became in England, in 1688, classic again, to drift gradually into democracy. In France, after 1793, it was at once artificial and sentimental. When Jeremy Bentham's ideas flourished in England, it became Utilitarian and preached the doctrines of common sense. When Bolingbroke reflected the tendencies of the time, it was affected with polite Deism. Bolingbroke furnished Voltaire with ideas. And France, in return, sent artificial tears and sentimental theories to the English Sterne.

Life acts and reacts through literature; it asserts and denies through literature. But who can say how far the vital book influences a people, and how far the people have influenced the vitality of a book? Literature forces the abstractions of the philosopher into the conduct of life. The pessimism of Schopenhauer is brought, through the novel, to our very hearthstones. The illusions of self-styled truth permeate our familiar companion, the daily newspaper. "Man," as Fierns-Gevaert says, in "La Tristesse Contemporaine" "thinks of himself as an equal co-worker with God; he believes that modern inventions supply oversights of the Creator in the beginning." One may find something of this in Rudyard Kipling. "All modernity," continues Fierns-Gevaert, "suffers for the lack of love. Our multiplied activities, our haste in work, the quickness in communication, the desire for long voyages and the ease with which they are accomplished, hasten to a speedy end the marked decadence of meditation."

Philosophical speculation and industrial changes affect the life of all classes, and literature expresses their effects. It seems only the other day as if the whole world was governed by pessimism, with literature as its prophet. The essay, the poem, the novel, even the little lyric spoke of gloom and of hopeless gloom. Studied rationally as a manifestation of the psychology of life,— of the psychology of the individual, as well as of the psychology of a people,— literature gives the clue to the problem. But what method can be supplied to humanity to tell us when the action will end, in any movement, and the reaction begin? And until we can find some scientific means of discovering the laws that govern the flux and reflux of human minds, we must be content to use literature as a working test. When the various human phenomena are explained, there will be no need to examine literature apart from this explanation. The limitations of life bar out the analysis of literature aside from life. One limitedly explains the other; and just as a single phase of literature seems fixed, a reaction or a revolt begins. "Romance, the root of all evil, is dead, the pernicious ideal is dead," Zola exclaimed triumphantly, not very long ago; "the dreams of the poor are gone, the legends of the saints and heroes are gone — science, as expressed by the realist, is the meaning of the modern world!"

Suddenly there is a change. The civilized world plunges into a sea of romance. The realistic rats and the pumpkin of Cinderella are changed to the apparatus of splendor in a moment. Is "Cyrano de Bergerac" or "Ulysses" a cause or an effect? This much is certain; its idealism has found a ready response from the heart of life. Pessimism goes out; the dilettanti even smile again. In Paris it is said aloud that God may no longer fear that He may not be believed in. Science no longer talks of analyzing the seraphim. Zola lays sacrilegious hands on the tabernacle of the spiritual life. The world all at once finds him ridiculous. Literature reflected the change from blatant doubt to mystical reverence, and concentrated the rays of the new light. How powerful it is in its action upon life, and how sensitive to every change in the tendencies of life!

The wizard waves his wand, and we forget or are consoled. High to heaven we go with St. John, or down to hell with Dante. We have left for a time the chill of earth's wind. Life demands this — and the demand is a cry for immortality. Literature answers the demand, for literature is a servant and a master of life.

THE EBB AND FLOW OF ROMANCE

THE EBB AND FLOW OF ROMANCE

EVERYBODY finds it easier to describe than to define the word "romantic" as applied sometimes to the Homeric books, oftentimes to Mademoiselle de Scudéry's "Grand Cyrus," and always to Sir Walter Scott's poems and novels. And most arguments about the meaning of this term end, as they end in Alfred de Musset's "Lettres de Dupuis à Cotonet," in a series of contradictions.

Of late, interest in the philosophical and social forces that affect literary movements seems to have increased among persons busy about other things. And the excuse for this essay — which contains the essential points of several lectures for students — is that it is meant as an answer to several questions from such persons.

That the romantic movement and the reactions from it were dependent on philosophical, social, and political influences is obvious. That they were not always conscious — not always the result of rules or formulated principles — seems quite as evident.

It is easy to prove that in the Golden Age of Spanish literature the literary movement was not a conscious, philosophical movement.

The epoch of the drama in Spain — that epoch which Cervantes, Lope de Vega, and Calderon made, and which lasted about one hundred years — was romantic. It was romantic both in spirit and in form. The famous plays of Cervantes, "Numantia" and "The Captives of Algiers," disregard all classical rules. Cervantes did for the Spanish stage what Corneille did for the French, — he fixed its best elements; and Lope de Vega, his successful rival, carried on the work which Calderon's masterpieces finally completed. The seventeenth century, in the beginning of which Shakespeare died, saw, in Spain, Cervantes found a new school of novelists with "Don Quixote," and likewise pave the way, in the drama, for the wonderful Lope de Vega and the still more wonderful Calderon.

In France Corneille borrowed largely from Spanish material, he remained classical both in feeling and form; and Racine, more human, more sympathetic, was almost an abject slave to the French versions of the rules of Aristotle. Corneille was so Roman in his feeling, and so imitative of the models furnished by Seneca, that it has been truly said that, as a rule, " all his men are demigods and all his women men." Cervantes, Lope de Vega, Calderon, wrote as if the rules of Aristotle and the classical formulæ had never existed. They were as romantic as Victor Hugo, but they had merely to take episodes from the life around to make thrilling incidents in a comedy of the cloak and sword, or in that more heroic species of drama which answers to our idea of tragedy.

Webster's Elizabethan romantic play, " The Duchess of Malfi," which is made up principally of ghosts and murderers, is not more regardless of the classical rules or more romantic than Cervantes' " Numantia " or Calderon's " The Physician of His

Own Honor." Previous to Cervantes, the imitators of Italy — the believers in imitation, which is the essence of classicism — had held sway; but Cervantes turned to the people and reflected the taste of the proud, fantastic, yet grave and religious Spaniard. He succeeded, he tells us, in such measure that during the progress of at least thirty of his plays not even a cucumber or an orange — missiles used against the unpleasing comedians of the Spanish theatre — was thrown upon the stage! Comedy, in the Spanish sense, was not comedy in the sense of Molière, — a play of manners ending happily. It might be a very serious drama, religious in motive, grave in method, yet not without comic incidents. Cervantes changed it from four to five acts. From the Spanish point of view, "The Merchant of Venice" and "Measure for Measure" are comedies, though the Elizabethan would probably have called them tragicomedies and the French critics of the eighteenth century refused to classify them except as barbarous.

Lope de Vega frankly says that he followed the tastes of the people. The king or the coterie had very little to do with him. He was, although he knew thoroughly all the classical dicta, entirely democratic. No plot was too intricate nor episode too improbable for him. And "The Wonderful Magician" of Calderon well shows how passionately romantic, how disdainful of the classical autocrats, the last great master of the Spanish drama was. The Golden Age of Spanish literature was romantic and democratic. It was, as Heine says of literature in general, "a mirror of life." It was not a conscious revolt against imitation or arbitrary rules. Lope de Vega put it naively when he said that he "gave the people what they paid for."

The religious side — deep, essential, fervent — of the Spanish people was not left out of their dramas. This romantic time has left some wonderful religious pieces, which must grow in the estimation of critics the better they are known. There are the "Autos Sacramentales" of Lope de Vega and Calderon. Cervantes was the first to conceive, for dramatic purposes, the soul of man as a little world, in which all the emotions, passions, aspirations, sins — supernatural grace itself — are personified. The origin of the Spanish theatre was not religious, though, like all theatres, it expressed religion when the people were religious. The religious drama, " Sacramental Acts," — splendid, elevated, as rich in poetry and colored language as the studded background of a Byzantine Madonna is in gems, — is a distinct expression of the personal and national spirit of Spain. The form of the " Autos " is romantic. They represent the religious drama at its highest point, and they could only come from and appeal to a people to whom the teachings of religion were not only familiar but vitally interesting. They are no wild, semi-barbarous miracle-plays or moralities, but works of art and poetry, touched with divine fire. They are the product of trained theologians and philosophers, and they appeal to no illiterate people. They represent a special phase of the religious romantic literary movement.

If the poetry of Chaucer is romantic in spirit, it is only so in the sense that it was bound to no narrow treatment of subject or to no fixed models of imitation outside the poet's intellectual taste. The introduction to "The Canterbury Tales" is realistic. No modern novel could, in the best sense, be more so. "The Knight's Tale" is romantic, if you will, because it clothes the Greeks of the old legends with the panoply of the Middle Ages. Theseus, the Greek, becomes a Duke, and the apparatus of the story of Arcite is brought down to the point of view of the fourteenth century. If we call Chaucer romantic because he represented life as he saw it and delighted in his own time, why not call Homer romantic?

"Chaucer's pages," says Professor Beers in his "History of English Romanticism in the Eighteenth Century," "abound with tournaments, hunting parties, baronial feasts, miracles of saints, feats of magic; but they are robed as well with the everyday life of the fourteenth-century England." Here we have romanticism and realism touching. And if we apply, as we may, the spirit of Professor Beers's words to Homer, we must admit that the chief of all Greek poets is a classic without being more classical than Chaucer, and that, at least in his picture of Odysseus and the lovers of Penelope, he was as romantic as Sir Walter Scott.

The drama of England down to the Restoration was frankly romantic. There was no conflict between the classical and romantic schools, though Ben Jonson doubtless sighed over Shakespeare's romanticism when he admitted that the author of "Hamlet" had little Latin and less Greek. It is certain that Shakespeare did not trouble himself about the rules of Aristotle, and that there were no critics in his audience who objected to the form of "The Merchant of Venice" as unclassical. Dryden might have done so; but in the latter part of the sixteenth century Dryden had not yet begun to be the first of English professional critics. As it is, it is to his credit that when, under the French influence of the Restoration, Shakespeare had almost been forgotten, he raised even a timid plea for him. But after 1688 — the year of Pope's birth and the beginning of constitutional government in England — classicism came into fashion.

The Italian conceits and the euphuisms of Sir Philip Sidney and Surrey, carried to excess, had been ridiculed by Shakespeare and were out of fashion; and so were the spontaneity, the freshness, the love of the natural man, which had distinguished Shakespeare and the best of his contemporaries. Addison and Pope gave the tone to verse and prose; and, reticent as it was, the apotheosis of the commonplace as it was, it showed a healthy reaction against the false sentiment and unbridled license of the years of Charles II and James II. It was such prose and verse as comfortable deists might write, — deists who would consider the Apocalypse an exaggeration in bad form, and the death of a Christian martyr as a very shocking performance, which a grain of incense gracefully dropped before a well-modelled god would have prevented. Romance was out of fashion; for romance meant aspiration and unrest, an interest in the past, a reaction against the present; and Addison and Pope and others were quite willing, before the comfortable fires of their favorite coffee-houses, to believe that "whatever is, is right."

If Pope and Addison were aristocratic and classical, "icily regular, splendidly null," they preceded an era of democracy.

The time when Addison could assume the mantle of Dryden and become an autocrat of literature was rapidly passing. The day of the patron was passing. The great Dean Swift might go about among his noble friends extorting guineas for his "little Papist poet, Pope"; but the years were at hand when historians, poets, and all book-makers were to appeal to the people, not to a coterie. The Hôtel de Rambouillet and the year 1600 were gone forever; the ladies whose criticisms made or unmade Corneille, who encouraged the young Bossuet, and who displaced a court preacher because they could whisper to that arbiter of letters, the Cardinal Richelieu, that he used non-academic words, had passed like the snows of last year. The time was coming when the democratic idea, which did not concern itself with kings and princes, was to find expression in letters and to dominate. In France it came out in the romantic revolt of Victor Hugo; from 1774 until his time it had been as sordid in letters as the Marats and Robespierres who let loose the hurricane of revolution. It was an appeal of the individual to individuals.

In France it was a conscious revolt, with principles and a formula. In England it expressed itself in a new vein of history, but, first, in the novels of Fielding and Smollett.

Shakespeare could not conceive a man heroic who had not noble blood. So sure of this was he that his first object when he went back to Stratford a rich man was to restore the family arms. Hamlet was a prince, Rosalind the daughter of a duke, Macbeth a patrician of his land, Perdita the daughter of a king, Portia of a great caste in Italy, and Romeo high among his people. Fielding changed all this, and the hero of the first great novel of the eighteenth century is a foundling. Moreover, Fielding holds the mirror up to nature. He is a realist, but he does not proclaim himself so. The time, as he pictured it, is a coarse and animal time, when religion had ceased to be more than a name for a comfortable belief that the Supreme Being would never think of damning anybody who paid an income tax. The comfortable middle classes began to reign.

The novels of Miss Austen and Miss

Edgeworth preceded those of Anthony Trollope, and have been succeeded by those of Howells and James. You can trace the line of realism back to Defoe. With Howells and James realism is conscious and analytical. Nevertheless, it is an imitation of the French philosophy of the realistic, while in succession to the spontaneous realism of Miss Austen; the latter answered to a demand from society, as Richardson's literary pap, flavored with Rousseau's rosewater and named "Clarissa Harlowe," had answered to a demand for a more sympathetic knowledge of human nature. Richardson was vocal of the democratic movement, though he probably despised it as much as he despised the principles of Rousseau.

In history Gibbon's "Decline and Fall of the Roman Empire," with its elaborate pagan paraphernalia and constant march of processional sentences, showed that history aimed to be literature. But it is to Macaulay we owe the development of the democratic movement into history. Macaulay says:

"The historians have imposed on themselves a code of conventional decencies as absurd as that which has been the bane of the French drama. The most characteristic and interesting circumstances are omitted or softened down, because, as we are told, they are too trivial for the majesty of history. The majesty of history seems to resemble the majesty of the poor king of Spain, who died a martyr to ceremony because the proper dignitaries were not at hand to render him assistance."

The historian was no longer to write of kings and princes and battles, leaving the people, like dim spectres, to stand in the distance. It may have been that, with the exit of the Stuarts, kings had ceased to be picturesque. And if it be a choice between principle and the picturesque, literature is drawn to the picturesque as the metal to the magnet. At any rate, English democracy, nurtured at the time of King John and the Magna Charta, had slowly come to maturity. Macaulay, at any rate, turned to the people, to the private and public records of daily life. Literature was to become more and more the expression of humanity, and it followed the movement toward the people and from the people. Macaulay himself expressed his theory of the historian's changed point of view, and faithfully put this theory into practice. The memoir, the diary, the letter, became material for the writer of history. It was no longer a question of the progresses of Louis XIV or of the plan of Waterloo; the lives of the men who fought, the social condition of the families that stayed at home, — all these are now things for the new investigation. The legend of Stephenson sitting by his mother's fire and discovering the action of steam replaces the story of King Alfred and the burned cakes in the neat-herd's hut; the picture of Franklin and his kite found more admirers than that of the foolish Canute and the advancing waves. In fact, the waves soused the king; and if a monarch had burned his cakes, the people saw no reason why he should not eat them or go without. Macaulay's method was exaggerated by Froude, with whom history became the personal expression of untruth. History to-day concerns itself with humanity; it may be called the psychology of the people, and the people are no longer incarnate in the person of the king.

The poet, however, remains a democrat

just as long as democracy can be made picturesque. The novelist, however, has a wider range, and is not so dependent on the picturesque. The novel was still realistic, — that is, it concerned itself with the probable in everyday life, until Sir Walter Scott arose. There had appeared tentative romances, like Horace Walpole's and Mrs. Radcliffe's, but they were lurid phantasmagorias. Sir Walter loved the past, and a century that was bounded by such an unpicturesque event as the Reformation irked him. The stirring Border Ballads rang in his ears. Besides, the cult of Goethe had tinged him with German romanticism. Between John Knox, grim, Hebraic, colorless, rude, denouncing the "Sabbath" afternoon dances of Mary Stuart, and Mary, radiant, gay, distinguished, candid, and a queen, he was all for Mary. Luther's vulgarity shocked him, and Calvin's pretensions filled him with contempt. Cromwell had good points for a romance, but those good points were visible only against a background of chivalry. It must be confessed that dear old Sir Walter loved the glamour of courts, the clash of arms, and the panoply of feudalism. But he also loved the Gothic tracery of high-pointed spires, and all the old world of which the cathedral and the abbey were the centre. And he loved, too, the creatures who would not have been what they were if it had not been for the old, yet ever new, religion. It would be untrue to say that Sir Walter consciously began a new movement in literature when he wrote "The Lady of the Lake" or that more influential work, "Waverley." He simply followed his bent; he liked the telling of a story so much that, in his declining days, the labor he delighted in physicked pain, and helped him to the highest heroism. "Peveril of the Peak" and "The Bride of Lammermoor," Edward Glendenning and the terrible Templar of "Ivanhoe" were of the company he cherished.

The ideal was never so obscured in England, religion never so much of a social convention, utilitarianism so prevalent and Philistinism so self-conceited, as in the beginning of the nineteenth century. The Reformation which had apotheosized the commonplace had cut off the English from their ancestors. The glory of the elder day was forgotten or ignored. It is hard for us to realize the interest excited by the appearance of Sir Walter Scott's novels, — the memoirs of the time show that the "Wizard of the North" was the most talked of person in Great Britain. The reign of the romance had come. Realism, so far as it concerned itself with everyday life in England, was out of fashion. Utilitarianism gave way, at least in theory, to aspiration. To fly upward was the motto; to get beyond the narrow walls of the present was the desire.

Few writers on Christianity have acknowledged its debt to the imagination. They have tried, following the lead of the reformers, to support it by common sense, when the fact is that the highest form of religion has as little to do with common sense as it has with the stock-market. The apostle who made himself "a fool for Christ's sake" was as much beyond the understanding of the average man of common sense as the ordinary reader of cheap magazines is below the poet of the Apocalypse. Sir Walter Scott, pioneer of the movement of aspiration, used the form of prose and the form of the novel; he was fortunate in that; the imagination of England caught fire. He showed that there were forgotten splendors in English faith and love. He re-peopled the cathedral and the abbey; he showed that the England of the Middle Ages was not the England of Fox's "Book of Martyrs." He cast aside the curtains of the commonplace, and the English beheld a new world all their own. The heroism they had lost so long, the romance hidden from them, appeared under the wand of the wizard:

> That through one window men beheld the Spring,
> And through another saw the Summer's glow,
> And through a third the fruited vines arow,
> While, still unheard, but in its wonted way,
> Piped the drear wind of that December day.

Men were glad to get out of the wind of the cold December and to feel the glow of the Spring. A return to chivalry meant a return to the Church. Gradually the movement grew, and we have Cardinal Newman's own testimony to the value of Sir Walter Scott's influence on the re-reading of English history. The progress to the Church, in which Newman was so distinguished a figure, would have come, — for ignorance could not always prevail. But there can be no doubt that the romantic movement in literature, which Sir Walter Scott both led and responded to, softened the temper of the English by broadening their views and illuminating their imagination.

In France the romantic movement of 1830 was a revolt, and a conscious revolt, against classic literary forms. Romanticism with Scott was a question of subject, of atmosphere; with Victor Hugo it was a question of form. "Romanticism," Brunetière says, speaking of the movement in France, "was not only a revolt, but a revolt made in order to uphold in honor all that classicism had, if not dogmatically condemned, at least effectually rejected. Romanticism is the ardor of incorrectness," as opposed to classicism, which, according to Brunetière, is "the regularity of good sense, the perfection of symmetry." Heine makes the essence of romanticism consist of allegory and aspiration; he speaks for that German point of view that had influenced Scott.

Hugo's romanticism was certainly a

disorder of the imagination, — violent because it was not only a rebellion against conventional and traditional rules, but in opposition, because the French bourgeois, commonplace and self-satisfied, were as unspiritual as the English Philistines. The English middle classes that could be satisfied to look on Benjamin West as a great painter were no better than the bourgeois that acclaimed David and Horace Vernet. Hugo was abnormally revolutionary. "Notre Dame de Paris" is a monstrous vision inspired by the frightful chimeras that keep watch from the roof of the old cathedral of many memories. Alexandre Dumas was more deeply influenced by Scott than Hugo. Hugo represented psychological reaction against the classical; the romantic France, before Richelieu and Louis XV, charmed him; he threw himself into a great open space and narrowly missed chaos. Dumas was a story-teller before all, — regardless of the probable, but with the power of making the impossible seem probable.

In all things the French go fast. It does not take them long to work out a problem. Lafayette's sentimental statement of the premises of the Revolution and the way they worked it out shows that. The revolt of Hugo against literary conventions did not stop with "Notre Dame de Paris" or with his drama, "Hernani." Dumas was an episode, influenced by Scott and answering a demand from France for fairy tales of the past. Dumas founded no school; he told his stories, and all France listened to them. They were exciting, and it was easy to see Anne of Austria and Cardinal de Retz and the celebrities of the Fronde through his glasses. As an artist, he was less hampered by the facts of history than even Scott. If D'Artagnan must die in one chapter, why not bring him to life in the next? He belonged to that school to which Sir Walter Scott has a suspicious leaning, — he was capable of making his heroine sea-green, if such a proceeding could add to the dramatic effect. There is no doubt, however, that he was as potent in the art of story-telling as was Sir Walter, and he held his hearers spellbound. While he wrote, there was no room for other romancers.

But against the revolution of Victor

Hugo there soon rose another revolt.
Romanticism cloyed, — the dungeons and
donjons of " La Tour de Nesle " and the
horrors of the old street of Paris were as
dreams. There was a demand for pictures of the present and of real life. As in
England Thackeray and Dickens, George
Eliot and Mrs. Gaskell came after the romantic arrival of Sir Walter Scott, so in
France the realists came after Hugo and
Dumas.

The movement in England was a
gentle and gradual movement. Thackeray was the literary descendant of the
realist Fielding and the sentimentalist
Sterne. Dickens owed something to a
much lesser man, the elder Pierce Egan;
and the difference in their earlier methods
shows the difference in their preceptors.
In France the realists announced a new
philosophy. Balzac was not a mere teller
of stories — " the idle singer of an empty
day " — he was an analyst, a psychological investigator. His mission was to
sound the depth of all humanity. The
novel was no longer to be a romance;
only the probable was possible. Balzac
wanted to be taken seriously; he was the

high priest of a new cult; so long as men and women existed, he could write — the inmost thoughts, emotions, virtues, sins of his time should be laid bare.

Honoré de Balzac was by no means a republican; he was an aristocrat, and he always allowed his people — he even encouraged them — to believe in God. He had the methods of the realist, and hence his contemporaries declared that he was a realist, for literary form is everything in France. But his heart was the heart of a romancer. His *mise en scène* is as realistic as Dickens's, but he is often as romantic and grotesque as Dickens. Still, he is held in France to have begun that misnamed realistic movement which ought to have had for its motto, "Anything that the devil does we shall deem it our mission to exaggerate." Realism, analytical realism, was acclaimed tumultuously. Balzac, the De Goncourts, Flaubert, followed one another. England already had realists as to method — Thackeray, Dickens, George Eliot; and a realist who pretended nothing, who assumed nothing, who had no relations with the French school, but who belonged to the school of

Miss Austen. This was Anthony Trollope. It was truly said of him that so long as men and women of the English upper-middle classes lived, he could go on writing. "Barchester Towers" and "Orley Farm" are the most typical examples of English realism, after "Pride and Prejudice," in our language. Mr. Howells and Mr. James have given us other good examples, tinged somewhat with the self-consciousness of the French, — "A Modern Instance," "The Rise of Silas Lapham," "The Portrait of a Lady," and "Washington Square." Of these, "Silas Lapham" seems to show most plainly the influence of Balzac.

Realism itself could not escape analysis; the newer man wanted to dry it as the chemist dries alcohol. Every drop of water must disappear. And then the Darwinian movement was affecting life. Realism, after all, cannot escape being synthetical, since even the most scientific of the new school was forced to call in the aid of imagination. Here was the difficulty. Besides, Balzac — even the all-seeing Balzac — hesitated to say some things; Flaubert had his reserves. The movement of realism was hampered by prudery, and it was not sufficiently "scientific." Zola, instead of being the founder of a school, is the beginning and the end of an illogical attempt in literature to dig around the roots of animal life in search of the monstrous grubs that infest the animals. The naturalistic-scientific movement somewhat affected Matilda Serao in Italy and the clever Spanish novelists, among whom are Galdos and Madame Pardo-Bazan. In England it touched George Moore. In Russia it influenced Tolstoi and Dostoeffsky. It has had no permanent effect, except upon D'Annunzio, who may call himself a pathological criminologist of the scientific-naturalistic school. Literature, one sees, has for some time been forging cheques upon the Bank of Science, just as that bank was engaged in playing the same game with the Bank of Theology.

In the drama — which the aristocratic and classical French Academy and the Théâtre Français had carefully guarded until Hugo broke down all conservatism with "Hernani" — the physiological problem play of the younger Dumas was followed by a great horde of dramas, all analyzing the relations of the sexes. In manner they were exquisitely technical. As to theatrical method, no stage has ever reached the height of the French in the last thirty years. But no stage, except that of the Restoration in England, was ever so degenerate. It affected the theatres of the whole civilized world. It helped to produce the gloomy Hauptmann in Germany and the gloomier sex-problemist in Norway, Ibsen. It was so brilliant that the English and Americans, who have no opinions of their own on art, could only translate and imitate. Its force is spent, and the French theatre of to-day, like Italian art, makes bric-à-brac, and that of a frivolous kind. There are two men in France, however, who have redeemed the French stage, — Henri de Bornier and Edmond Rostand, who wrote the "Daughter of Roland" and "Cyrano de Bergerac."

With "Cyrano" has come in France a tendency to idealism and romanticism. There can be no doubt that a new literary reaction was badly needed. "Cyrano" was a dramatic success, not because it was great, but because everybody of sanity and taste was disgusted by the public presentment of problems which neither the literature of the stage nor any literature could solve, and which could only show literature as impotent and degraded. "Cyrano" has another meaning, too, but only a limited and narrow one. It represents that symbolistic movement which has not yet reached the modern literature of any other country. It can be fully understood only by those who know the history of the movement of preciosity under Cardinal Richelieu and the coterie of Madame de Rambouillet in France. We all remember how Molière laughs at this in "Les Précieuses Ridicules," and how Shakespeare smiles at the English counterpart in the character of Osric, in "Hamlet." The chief of the symboliste movement in France is Henri de Regnier; he is an amateur of jewelled words, a maker of sonnets which are mosaics of sound. He is a rebel against realism and literary naturalistic science. He and his school appeal to the senses rather than to the mind; each word has its peculiar perfume, each cadence is intended to arouse a mood, each pause puts the climax to an emotion; if you know how precious the aroma of words is, how vital the cadence of sounds to the receptive mind, you can understand why Roxane fell in love with opaline phrase and the ruby-tinted sentence and the emerald word, and left out entirely the human being. Symbolism is part of the reaction against vulgar realism. The symbolist, who slept with the swine when he was a naturalistic realist, cannot now endure a crumpled rose leaf.

In English-speaking countries the scientific-realistic movement has spent its force. Reverence and mysticism are coming into vogue again, and with them the romance. A man who does not to-day assume that he would like to believe, if he could, is as much out of the fashion as the man who doubted Spencer or Huxley twenty-five years ago. And the more you believe, the more you are in the current of the stream. It is the old motion of the pendulum. Therefore the romance is king. Poetry is even coming into vogue; the poets are struggling out of their twilight, and it will soon be day for them.

Everybody that is rich looks around for ideals, and everybody that is not rich hopes to acquire some as soon as he can afford to keep them.

In the fine arts we have been much affected by a movement which is partly literary. It was a stream flowing from the great romantic river of the beginning of this century — the river of romanticism that helped to fertilize the Tractarian fields.

The Preraphaelite reaction meant the saving of England from Philistinism. It was a revolt against the unintellectual conventions that had stifled the beautiful in England. Ruskin, who, if he had lived a hundred years, would have died too soon, gave it force in literature and in the art of painting; Tennyson exemplified it in his earlier poems; Dante Gabriel Rossetti expressed it in his verses and pictures. The intensity of the movement, its archaism, its affectations, almost sent the pendulum swinging back to Philistinism; but the education of the people had gone too far. The admiration for the great masters before Raphael, the demand of Ruskin that all artists should seek the beautiful in nature and depict it naturally, the accepting of simple forms, differentiated and distinct, in preference to the artificial symbols of nature which conventional painters had used unreflectingly, were essentials of this movement. The influence of this Preraphaelite movement spent itself in literature with "The Blessed Damozel" and "The Earthly Paradise." But in the art of painting, especially in the revival of the older forms of beauty for household decoration, the Preraphaelite revolt has been very potent.

The clue to the romantic reaction — by which the Oxford movement was vitalized and from which the Preraphaelites had their being — is thus named by W. J. Courthope in "The Liberal Movement in English Literature":

"If we are simply and solely positive, we shall not be able to create at all. The exclusive scientific order, which the philosophers who have appropriated the title of Positive would impose on society, is more remote from the reality of nature, or, at least, of human nature, than the wildest extravagances of the Arabian Nights. The revolt of the romantic school against the excessive realism of the eighteenth century ought to prove, *a fortiori*, that men will not tolerate an intellectual system from which the mystical and religious element is altogether excluded."